D1568002

Glass Buildings

Heinz W. Krewinkel

Glass Buildings

Material, Structure and Detail

Birkhäuser
Basel · Berlin · Boston

This publication was kindly supported by Robert Danz, GÖTZ GmbH and Pilkington Deutschland GmbH.

Translation into English by Gerd H. Söffker and Philip Thrift

Library of Congress Cataloging-in-Publication Data

A CIP catalogue record for this book is available from the Library of Congress, Washington D.C., USA

Die Deutsche Bibliothek – CIP Einheitsaufnahme

Krewinkel, Heinz W.: Glass buildings : material, structure and detail / Heinz W. Krewinkel. [Transl. into engl. by Gerd Söffker and Philip Thrift]. – Basel ; Berlin ; Boston ; Birkhäuser, 1998
Dt. Ausg. u.d.T.: Krewinkel, Heinz W.: Glasarchitektur
ISBN 3-7643-5650-2 (Basel ...)
ISBN 0-8176-5650-2 (Boston)

© 1998 Birkhäuser – Publishers for Architecture,
P.O. Box 133, CH-4010 Basel, Switzerland

This book is also available in a German language edition (ISBN 3-7643-5649-9).

Printed on acid-free paper produced from chlorine-free pulp (TCF).

Design and typography:
Martin Schack/Alexandra Schaffer, Dortmund

Illustration on page 2: Art gallery, Bregenz

Printed in Germany

ISBN 3-7643-5650-2

ISBN 0-8176-5650-2

9 8 7 6 5 4 3 2 1

Contents

6

Crown glass.

1 Molten glass is drawn out of the furnace with the blowing iron and formed into a pear shape on an iron plate. 2 Reheating, blowing and turning forms a "balloon". 3 When the balloon is large enough, the blowing iron is removed and replaced by an iron rod on the opposite side. 4 The balloon on the iron rod is reheated again. Rapid turning of the glass balloon, made ductile by the heating and open at the point where the blowing iron was broken off, causes the centrifugal force to push the edges outwards, thereby forming a circular disc. 5 Finished disc with small air bubble (bleb) in the centre where the iron rod is attached. 6 The red-hot discs cool down gently in a furnace in which the temperature slowly sinks.

Blown cylinder sheet glass.

1 The molten glass is drawn off with a blowing iron and preformed. 2 Reheated, the ductile glass is formed into a "balloon" with a flat base by blowing and turning.
3 Reheated again and again, a cylinder is produced by swinging the glass over a pit. The diameter is kept constant by blowing. 4 After cooling, the cylinder is cut open. 5 The opened cylinder is heated up so that it can be flattened out into a flat pane. Afterwards, the pane is slowly cooled.

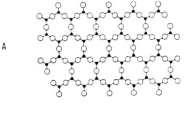

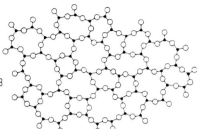

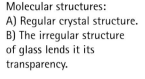

Molecular structures:
A) Regular crystal structure.
B) The irregular structure
of glass lends it its
transparency.

7

Architectural glass

As the oldest man-made material, glass can look back on a history spanning over 7,000 years. This fusion product, whose main constituent is sand (silicon dioxide, SiO_2), is characterized by its very singular properties. Best known of these is its transparency; less well known is the fact that glass is not a solid but rather a liquid solidified at room temperature. In the *Schott Glaslexikon* it is defined as follows: "Glass is a material the structure of which resembles a liquid whose viscosity at normal ambient temperatures is so high that it can be considered to be a solid. More strictly, the term 'glass' is applied to all inorganic compounds having this basic property. This distinguishes glass from the plastics family, all of which have an organic base and for this reason should not be referred to as glass even if they are transparent."

The comparison between glass and crystal which is often drawn might relate to the reflective and sparkling effects of the two materials, but in terms of physics is inappropriate. The molecular structure of a crystal is regular whereas that of glass is irregular; that is what makes glass transparent while a clear crystal might be translucent at best. One intrinsic property of glass is that it is inert, i.e. neutral with respect to its surroundings; it does not form any chemical compounds and its constituents do not separate. Its suitability for recycling also adds to its environmental compatibility.

On the other hand, glass is not simply glass! By adding various admixtures to the main constituent, silicon dioxide, various types of glass with very particular properties can be produced from the fusion product. Today, the flat glass most widely used for architectural purposes is a soda-lime glass whose properties of a non-porous surface and weathering resistance make it ideally suited to such use.

History

Egypt has provided the oldest glass found to date in the form of glass beads and vessels dated at about 5,000 BC. Glass was used in buildings from very early times, in the form of mosaics, but it was only after the invention of the blowing iron in the 1st century BC, probably in the Phoenician city of Sidon (in present-day Lebanon), that the production of transparent glass became feasible. With this marvellously simple tool – an iron tube about 1-1.5 m long with a 10 mm bore – it was

The viscosity of glass. All states are reproducible and reversible. Therefore, glass can be easily recycled.

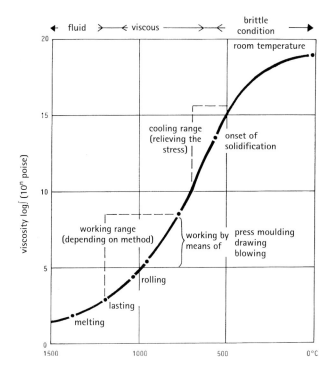

The table casting method for producing cast glass. The molten glass is poured onto a bed and rolled flat. Engraving according to Diderot and d'Alembert, 1773.

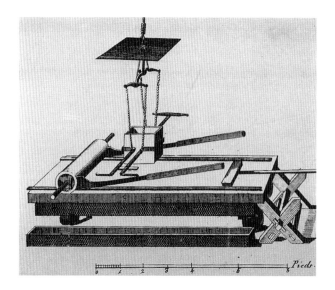

A schematic presentation of a float glass plant.

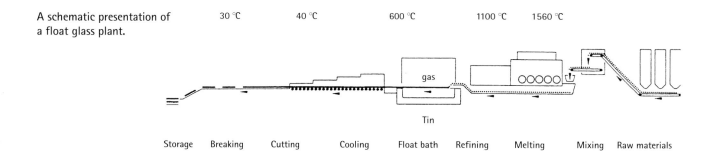

now possible to blow molten glass into a hollow vessel. This blowing iron has remained unchanged for 2,000 years and today is still a masterly tool in the hands of a skilled glassblower. In order to produce clear, transparent glass, it must not come into contact with cooler foreign substances at the moment of solidification. If this does happen, then a layer of premature solidification occurs at the point of contact which has a different refractive power to that of the inner layer. Such contact can be avoided with glass-blowing; the blown glass remains fire-polished.

Up until 1925 window glass was also formed by hand-blowing, initially hollow vessels but later cylinders which were then cut open and flattened out. After 1925 the industrial production of window glass using the drawing process developed by Emile Fourcault as well as Eduard Libbey and Michael Owens started to be widely used. In 1688 in France, Nicolaus de Nehou designed a method for the pouring of glass onto a bed where it was then rolled flat. Owing to the contact with the bed and the rollers, this cast glass is opaque. To obtain clear, transparent glass, the surfaces have to be ground and polished. The table casting method was used for 150 years to produce particularly even, distortion-free, flat glass, above all for mirrors. This method too was developed into a continuous production process.

The invention of the float glass technique around 1955 by Sir Alastair Pilkington of Pilkington Brothers plc in St Helens, England, put an end to the drawing method as well as the grinding and polishing of cast glass. The float glass technique allows the production of flat glass in a quality superior to that of drawn glass and equal to that of ground and polished cast glass. This makes the manufacturing process more rational. The float technique is based on the notion of floating the molten glass over an optimum surface in order to obtain fire-polished glass. Only a liquid offers the ideal surface for this; therefore, Pilkington floated his molten glass over a bath of liquid tin. At the point at which the glass enters, the liquid tin has a temperature of 1,000°C; tin is the only metal which fulfils the requirements of being a liquid at just 600°C but still not producing any damaging vapour pressure at 1,000°C. Today, tin baths for float glass are 60 m long. The ribbon of glass is drawn through by rollers mounted on the sides. The width of the ribbon produced is 3.21 m and the thickness depends on the speed at which the glass passes over the tin; thicknesses of 4-19 mm are common. These fully automatic float glass lines produce up to 3000 m^2/h at a thickness of 4 mm. A bath can operate continuously for up to about 15 years before a cold repair is necessary. At present there are more than 180 float glass lines in operation throughout the world, manufacturing the basic glass ready for further treatment to give it insulating, solar-control, acoustic and fire-resistant properties.

One special field has been the development of so-called safety glass, which grew out of the special needs of vehicle windscreens. In 1909 the French chemist Edouard Benedictus invented laminated safety glass by sandwiching a layer of celluloid between two panes of glass; the celluloid held the splinters of glass in place upon breakage. Today, the middle layer consists of a viscoplastic PVB sheet which lends the laminated glass a residual strength by bonding the splinters upon breakage. During the 1920s the Societé Anonyme des Manufactures des Glaces et Produits Chemiques de St Gobain, Chauny & Cirey, Paris, invented "Sekurit", a toughened (or tempered) safety glass. The glass is prestressed thermally by heating and then subsequently cooling it. This process cools the surfaces quicker than the inside of the glass, leaving the outer layers in compression and the core in tension. Glass prestressed in this way has a higher tensile bending strength (characteristic strength 50 N/mm^2 compared to 30 N/mm^2 for float glass) and also a better thermal fatigue resistance (temperature difference 150 K compared to 40 K for float glass). Upon breakage the prestress is released allowing the glass to disintegrate into tiny pieces (dice) at a velocity of 1500 m/s.

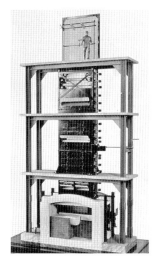

A glassblower in a French glassworks c. 1340.

A model of a glass drawing plant by Emile Fourcault in the Deutsche Museum, Munich.

A shorter prestressing process produces heat-treated glass (characteristic strength 40 N/mm^2) which although it has a higher tensile bending strength, still shatters like float glass upon breakage. This type of glass is employed in the manufacture of laminated safety glass where, on the one hand, the increased tensile bending strength is exploited and, on the other, large splinters in combination with the plastic interlayer ensure adequate residual strength.

Vehicle manufacture also saw the first use of multipane insulating glass formed by two or more identical or differing panes held at the edges by spacer pieces and sealed airtight. The intervening space is filled with dry air or noble gases like argon or krypton to give the construction its insulating properties. On 23 November 1934 Sicherheitsglas GmbH, Kunzendorf/Niederlausitz, was granted the German patent for the production method for a double-pane joined along the edges. This first double glazing was used in the fast railcars of German Railways at that time. However, it was not until 1951 that such glass found its way into buildings. In 1938 the insulating glass "Thermopane" was patented in the USA. Introduced into the German market in 1954, the name became an everyday term for insulating glass in general.

Glass in buildings

The Crystal Palace, London, by Sir Joseph Paxton, 1851.

After the Graeco-Roman and Byzantine glass mosaics, it was mainly in the great glass windows of Gothic cathedrals that glass started to influence buildings. However, glass architecture as such first began with the palm houses and glasshouses of the 19th century. The most prominent example was the Crystal Palace, designed by Sir Joseph Paxton for the Great Exhibition of 1851 in London. The 270,000 panes of glass of the "Palace of Industry for all Nations" were each a standard 1220 mm long, 254 mm wide and 2 mm thick. They were all hand-blown and at that time constituted one-third of England's total annual production of window glass! Besides palm houses and exhibition halls, glass was much in evidence in the architecture of the 19th century for glass arcades, station roofs and atria. And in the private sphere, conservatories enjoyed great popularity.

Glass architecture received a new impetus with the *Neues Bauen* (New Building) movement of the 1920s. Light, air and sunshine within the building were the ideals. Framework construction enabled generous areas of glazing. Curtain walls of glass and steel were first used in 1914 by Walter Gropius in his administration building design for the Fagus factory in Alfeld an der Leine in northern Germany. In 1926 Gropius designed the fully glazed workshop wing of the *Bauhaus* in Dessau; Le Corbusier followed in 1929 with his Salvation Army home in Paris, which has a fully glazed façade with no opening lights. That residential building was equipped with air-conditioning but climate control in these early glass buildings was not sufficiently well understood; shading and thermal insulation presented technical problems which glass could not overcome at that time. Ludwig Mies van der Rohe's 1920/22 competition designs for an office building adjacent Berlin's Friedrichstrasse Station went unnoticed by the jury. However, as well as entering architectural history, his designs created the prototype for tall office buildings in framework construction with fully glazed façades.

It was not until over 30 years later that such tall buildings became a reality, when air-conditioning ensured the necessary internal climate. The global energy crisis of the 1970s also induced the glass industry to develop energy-saving products which would reduce both the heating and cooling loads of buildings. Another task to be tackled was the "sick building syndrome" caused by air-conditioning. The result was the development of new façade and building concepts which attempted to achieve an intelligent combination of all the elements of thermal insulation and shading, natural lighting by means of daylight and natural ventilation to a greater extent than had been customary in the past. In doing so, modern, special glass types have secured glass a high status as a material. The trendsetters in these developments were always architects, who explored new paths and used the shortcomings to assert new demands. Building and the solving of new challenges will always include experimentation.

New technologies

In terms of construction, the trend in glass architecture is towards a reduction in the supporting structure. Glass roofs trussed with sag rods minimize the need for steel framing and increase the transparency. The same is true for façades. Besides tension rods underneath or behind, there are cable-lattice designs and systems of individual mechanical fixings (bolted or small plate, so-called "patch", fittings) which render possible delicate glass architecture. And the use of glass as a structural material is growing; the high compressive strength of glass (880-930 N/mm^2) can be readily exploited for this. The problems lie in the material's much lower tensile bending strength (30-90 N/mm^2) and the risk of spontaneous brittle fracture. This latter characteristic can be compensated for by using laminated safety glass, which ensures an adequate residual loadbearing capacity upon breakage. Many more studies, trials and results are necessary in the field of structural glazing. More than ever before, this requires open and constructive exchange between all those concerned. The technological evolution of glass has by no means been exhausted, and the future will bring new, special types of glass, such as electrochromic glass, which assumes a certain colour upon the application of an electrical voltage and hence reduces solar radiation transmittance.

Glass details

Every material permits tolerances to a varying degree during its integration in a structure. However, in the case of glass these are decidedly minimal. Glass may not be subjected to any constraints and cannot be altered during erection, especially if it is prestressed. Therefore, glass structures require extraordinary precision. As glass is normally employed for its transparency, it cannot conceal supporting constructions. Therefore, these should be appropriate to this elegant material. To accomplish good solutions in glass construction, a close and innovative collaboration between architect, engineer and contractor is indispensable.

Acknowledgements

Details of existing buildings, above all reliable information on the glass used, would have been virtually impossible to obtain without the assistance of those who contributed to the glass construction in these buildings. Therefore, I am indebted to all the architects, engineers and contractors who provided invaluable help during my research; in particular, Robert Danz, Schönaich; Brüder Eckelt & Co., Steyr; Josef Gartner GmbH, Gundelfingen; von Gerkan, Marg und Partner, Hamburg; GÖTZ GmbH, Würzburg; Helmut Fischer GmbH, Talheim; Kilian & Hagmann, Stuttgart; Pilkington Flachglas AG, Gelsenkirchen; Seele GmbH, Gersthofen; and VEGLA Vereinigte Glaswerke GmbH, Aachen.

   I also owe a special debt of gratitude to my copy editor Ria Stein. She proved to be a competent and understanding companion right from the start.

A design for a fully glazed office building adjacent Berlin's Friedrichstrasse Station. Ludwig Mies van der Rohe, 1920.

The Bauhaus in Dessau. Walter Gropius, 1926.

Plan of upper floor,
scale 1:1500.

Plan of ground floor,
scale 1:1500.

Airside elevation,
scale 1:1500.

Section through passenger
hall, scale 1:1500.

Airside façade. The glass is behind aluminium channel sections which are interrupted to form the word GRAZ.

Graz Airport
Florian Riegler, Roger Riewe

The history of Graz Airport at Thalerhof began in 1913 with the establishment of a military airfield, from which the first "flying machine" took off on 26 June 1914. The end of the "Dual Monarchy" in 1918 and the peace treaty of St Germain in 1919 put an end to military aviation. Even civilian aircraft were banned in Austria. Until the lifting of the ban and the establishment of Austria's domestic air travel network in 1925, the facilities were used by gliders. The Vienna-Graz-Klagenfurt route became the first civil use for the airfield at Thalerhof. The facilities were closed down for a second time in 1945 after the end of the Second World War and it was not until 1951 that Austria's second-largest city was once again opened to international air traffic. A new passenger terminal was completed in 1969 and after the runway had been extended several times, a Concorde was able to land there in 1981. In 1988 the number of passengers passing through Graz each year had already exceeded 250,000.

Therefore, a design competition was held in 1989 to extend and modernize the terminal and offices. This was won by the Riegler-Riewe practice with a design which allowed plenty of space for future expansion. The most important criterion for the structure and the layout was the forecast of passenger figures. In 1990 a figure of 700,000 for the year 2000 was predicted, based on a peak hourly rate of 1000 passengers. This peak hourly rate is decisive for calculating areas for check-in, waiting and arrivals zones as well as for the congestion normal at passport and customs controls. In view of the anticipated 700,000 passengers annually, a single-level solution was favoured in which check-in, waiting, arrivals, entrances and exits are all located on one floor; two-level designs are only worthwhile when the number of passengers exceeds one million. Of the existing buildings, only the control tower, part of the office block and the restaurant were retained. The passenger hall was demolished. The whole facility was only lengthened slightly, leaving the original planning zone free for future expansion. The airport structures were considerably widened and the roof lowered, primarily to save energy. In describing their solution to the brief, the architects wrote: "Our design concept was to arrange all functions in a clear and logical manner, among other things suppressing the plethora of signs and symbols which normally prevails at airports. Consequently,

Location
Graz-Thalerhof Airport, Austria

Client
Flughafen Graz
Betriebsgesellschaft

Architects
Florian Riegler, Roger Riewe,
Graz

Assistance
Manuela Müller, Wolfgang
Pittino, Reinhold Weichlbauer,
Gerhard Zehner

Consultants
DI Eigner – project management and site supervision

GEI, Vienna – building services

Dr Tomberger – thermal and
acoustic specialist

Lighting Design Vienna,
Wagner – Bartenbach

Fully glazed façade, forecourt
Glas- und Metallbau Temmel,
Graz

Glass façades
Brüder Eckel & Co. Glastechnik
Ges.m.b.H., Steyr

Date of completion
1994

Airside elevation

The fully glazed façade of
insulating glass facing the
forecourt.

the check-in area is already visible from the forecourt and further structures are recognizable from many different viewpoints. Therefore, all internal structures in the passenger handling area are only 2.7 m high and room heights just 4 m. The use of various façade designs is quite deliberate; for example, for departing passengers, a fully glazed façade forms the transition between forecourt and passenger hall. Incoming travellers recognize a façade in which the word GRAZ has been integrated. Behind this façade, between passenger zone and control tower, lies the airport administration and the General Aviation Terminal."

The two-storey administration wing is accessible from all sides. From the passenger hall, a glass-roofed passageway leads to the offices. Beyond this passageway, two glazed bridges provide a link to the first floor of the block. The ground floor is reserved for public functions, whereas the upper floor contains the offices of the airport administration, the Federal Department for Civil Aviation and airport security. The roof over the passenger hall opens out in a series of glass domes which create a daylight ambience in the interior of the building. Therefore, very light colours are employed in this area; the floor and ceiling have a light green hue in order to match the natural light green tint of the glass. In designing the artificial lighting, care was taken to ensure that the light sources did not upset this colour scheme. It is for this reason that only the pictograms – for instance, indicating escape routes – are lit from behind, while all other signs have frontal illumination. Commenting on their overall concept, the architects said: "In working out the design, right down to the details, it was always important to us to see the airport as an interchange, a transfer point. From car to plane, from plane to car. As straightforward as possible."

Three glass façades

The 4-m-high fully glazed façade facing the forecourt is a vertical wall of insulating glass consisting of two panes of toughened safety glass, each 10 mm thick, with a 16 mm cavity. Glass stiffeners of 3-ply laminated safety glass, 30 mm thick, are incorporated in the façade. The protruding centre panes of the stiffeners are connected to the vertical joints of the 2 x 4 m panes of the façade by means of countersunk screws fixed from the outside.

Check-in zone in passenger hall. On the right, the fully glazed wall facing the forecourt.

15

Glass passageway in administration block. The glazed bridges of the upper floor span over the public area on the ground floor. The glass walls on both sides have translucent, fixed glazing and clear glass to window areas.

Glass stiffeners stabilize the fully glazed wall facing the forecourt.

Isometric view, scale 1:10. Detail of double-skin façade facing the runway. Outside, 8 mm toughened safety glass with printed dot pattern; inside, insulating glass (6/16/6 mm); 146 mm cavity.

Isometric view, scale 1:10. Detail of glass façades of office wing. Outside, 12 mm laminated safety glass (2 x 6 mm) with translucent PVC interlayer; inside, 6 mm toughened safety glass; 16 mm cavity filled with krypton gas.

Isometric view, scale 1:5. Glass stiffeners of laminated safety glass are attached at the joints of the insulating glass panes of the forecourt façade. They are secured from the outside by means of screws.

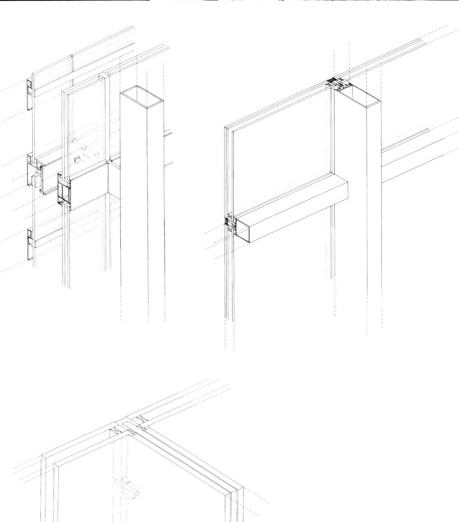

The glass façade on the airside is a 3-ply design, primarily to provide sound insulation. The inner skin comprises insulating glass (6/16/6 mm). The outer skin is 8 mm toughened safety glass printed with a fine pattern of dots. Placed in front of the outer pane is a grid of aluminium channel sections which incorporate the word GRAZ in negative. The spacing between inner and outer glass skins is 146 mm. All the outer panes are hinged for cleaning.

The façades to the offices are formed by insulating glass consisting of 12 mm laminated safety glass (2 x 6 mm) with opaque PVC interlayer (outer pane) and 6 mm toughened safety glass (inner pane). The cavity is filled with krypton gas. This "Starwhite" insulating glass has a k-value of 1.1 W/m^{2}K. It is a translucent, solar-control insulating glass which permits the construction of consistent, non-coloured glass walls and roofs. The panes with the opaque PVC interlayer offer privacy and scatter the incoming daylight. Windows are included where a view to the outside is practical and desirable.

It is important that the make-up of such functional glass types can also cover additional tasks specific to the project – especially important in airport design – such as sound insulation, intruder and bullet resistance. This is true for the three façades here. The terminal building at Graz is a good example of how building elevations need not be identical on all sides, as is traditionally the case. It is much more intelligent to arrange each elevation according to its function and orientation. In contrast to solid building materials, glass offers a multitude of possibilities in this respect.

Glass roof to Juval Castle, Staben
Robert Danz

The site of this castle on the rocky ridge between Etschtal and Schnalstal in the southern Tyrol is at an altitude of 927 m. From Staben itself, a paved road snakes up to the castle. Its builder is assumed to be Hugo von Montalban, who changed his name to Jufal after 1278. Soon afterwards, owners and occupants began to change frequently. Following its hey-day in the mid-16th century, its changing fate finally led to the collapse of the castle. In 1913 a Dutchman, William Rowland, bought the remains and began restoration work in 1925. After a further change of owner, the world-famous mountaineer Reinhold Messner purchased the castle site in 1983 and continued with the repairs. Since 1985 he has lived in Juval Castle with his family every year from spring to autumn. A glass roof was planned in order to protect the castle ruins beside the tower from further decay and to use the space to display Messner's collection. The Listed Buildings Authority agreed to the measures without any reservations as they contribute to preserving the structure.

Materials and design

The shape of the roof roughly corresponds to that of the former roof structure. With eaves projecting 250-400 mm beyond the rubble masonry walls and only a few points of support on the gable walls, the glass roof appears to float above the castle. Wall plates of HE-B 120 wide-flange I-section steel beams, galvanized and painted, are laid on the gable and side walls, anchored to the rubble masonry at several points. The fish-bellied girders spanning right across the space are attached to the wall plates. Adjacent the tower, the upper chord of each girder is let into the wall. The ridge of the roof runs from the south-east corner of the tower to the apex of the gable wall on the valley side. The structural calculations for the glass-and-steel construction were carried out according to the valid 1995 Building Code. However, the external walls of the north wing were excluded from this work as it was felt that the gable wall on the valley side had proved itself adequately stable through withstanding over 100 years of wind and other load! The top chords of the fish-bellied girders provide additional support for the gable wall. Extra bracing at roof level is not necessary because the plate effect of the glass panes already lends

Location
Schloss Juval, Staben, Italy

Client
Reinhold Messner, Meran

Designer and
structural engineer
Robert Danz, Schönaich

Site Manager
Prof. Dr.-Ing. Konrad
Bergmeister, Brixen, Vienna

Glass design
Delta-X GmbH,
Dr.-Ing. Albrecht Burmeister,
Stuttgart
Prof. Dr.-Ing. E. Ramm

Glass and steel construction
Gebrüder Fischnaller OHG,
Villnöss-Funez

Glazing
BGT Bischoff Glastechnik
GmbH, Bretten

Date of completion
1997

19

West side. A crane was set up on the tower for erecting the glass roof.

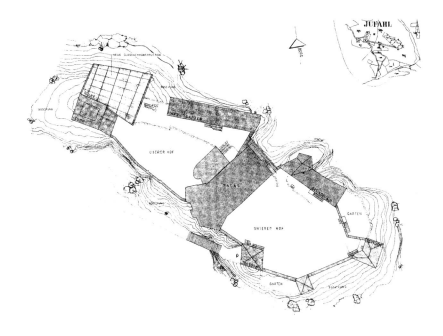

Site plan, scale 1:1000.

The castle stands on a rocky ridge between Etschtal and Schnalstal. The ruins of the upper section of the castle next to the tower were given a transparent glass roof to protect them.

sufficient stiffness and any bracing would be superfluous. The panes of glass span in the direction of the roof slope and have an overlapping joint along the axis of each steel beam.

As the roof surface is trapezoidal in plan, the panes of glass were laid out radially. The result of this is that no two pieces of glass are the same – not only the dimensions but the angles as well. The projection of the upper pane of the laminated safety glass beyond the lower pane at the overlapping edge, the eaves and the verge leads to further differences in the dimensions. All data was calculated with a CAD system in order to avoid mistakes during design and fabrication. This geometrical data was then transferred by floppy disk directly to the machines used for cutting and drilling the glass panes themselves. An essential prerequisite for

North elevation and section
A–A, scale 1:200.

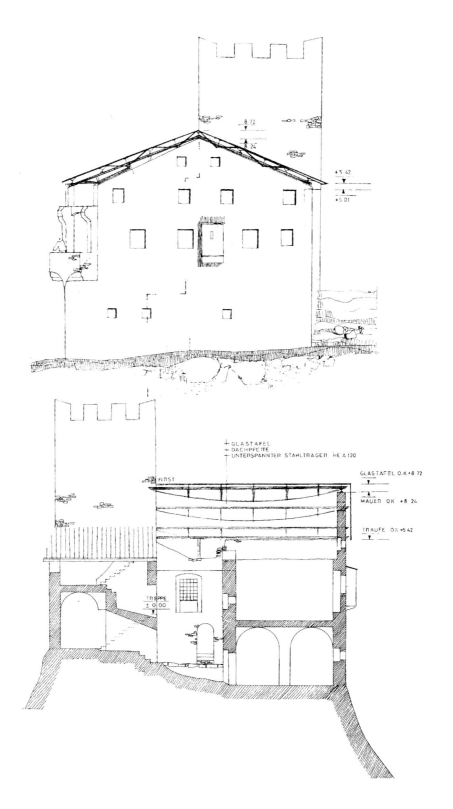

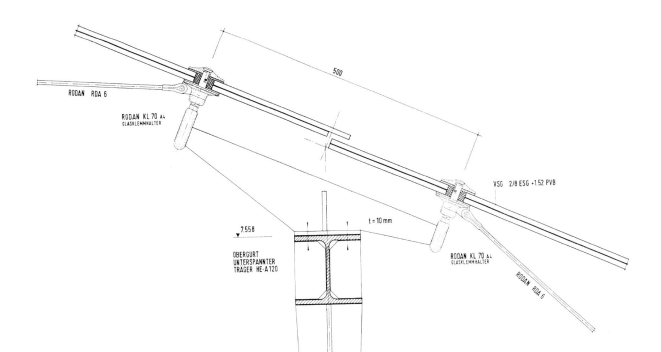

Fish–bellied girder,
scale 1:75.

RODAN RDA 6

RODAN KL 70 A4
GLASKLEMMHALTER

500

VSG 2/8 ESG +1.52 PVB

7.558

OBERGURT
UNTERSPANNTER
TRÄGER HE·A120

t = 10 mm

RODAN KL 70 A4
GLASKLEMMHALTER

RODAN RDA 6

Section through support on
top chord, scale 1:3,5.
The panes of glass overlap
each other like scales. The
joints are not sealed.

View towards the
south-east.

At the corner, the glass
cantilevers out over the
balcony.

Erecting the panes of glass
and steelwork by means of a
crane specially built for the
project and mounted on the
tower.

Plan of beam bearings,
scale 1:75.

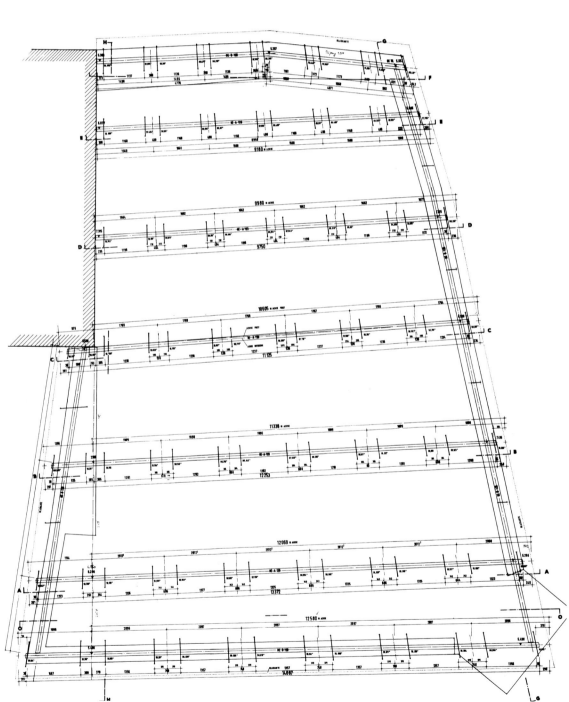

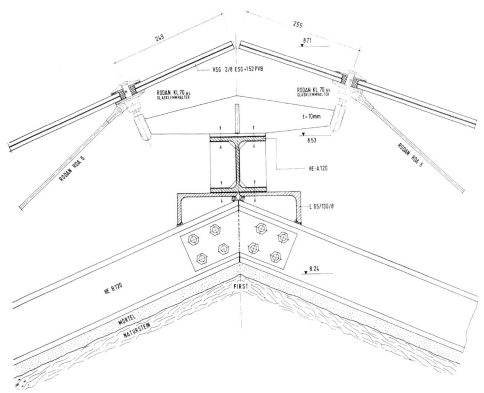

Wall plates of galvanized, wide-flange steel beams (HE-B 120) were placed on the northern gable wall. The fish-bellied girders spanning across the space are fixed to the wall plates. The trussed glass panes of laminated safety glass are fastened with individual bolted fixings.

Sectional elevation of ridge at gable wall, scale 1:7,5.

such work was an accurate survey (max. 3 mm tolerance) of the existing wall copings prior to the start of the design.

For architectural reasons, and also to convey the impression of an enclosed space, "Parsol" body-tinted, green transparent glass was chosen for the bottom pane of the laminated safety glass. The sizing of the glass panes and steelwork is based on a load of 185 kg/m² for snow and dead load. The glass used is a laminated safety glass comprising two 8 mm panes of toughened safety glass and a 1.56 mm PVB interlayer. The glass was subjected to an eight-hour heat-soak test. The trussed arrangement meant that the residual strength of the glass upon breakage did not need to be investigated as the ties guarantee sufficient stability for the splinters of glass held in place by the viscoplastic PVB interlayer – long enough to ensure that the danger area can be vacated in good time. The trussed panes of glass supported on gimbals on balance arms cover an area of about 200 m². The patented Rodan glass clamp mountings give the glass a statically determinate support and were able to be installed without inducing secondary bending moments. The glass clamp mountings enable tolerances to be compensated for in the X, Y and Z directions during erection. Even angular twist can be dealt with via this ball-bearing support. The larger hole in the pane of glass was filled with a special two-component epoxy resin ("epple RODAN contact") after erection in order to produce a positive but flexible connection between glass and mounting. Besides extensive structural calculations for the trussed glass panes by the Delta-X engineering practice, a full-size assembly also had to be tested in order to gain approval.

Exploded view of main
elements.

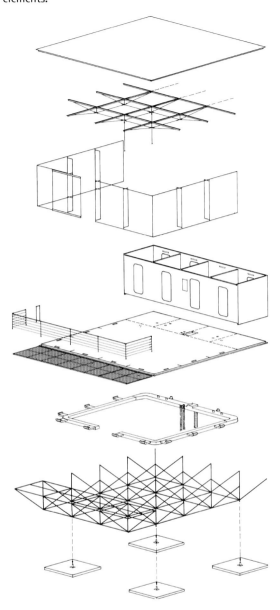

Horizontal and vertical detail
sections, scale 1:10.

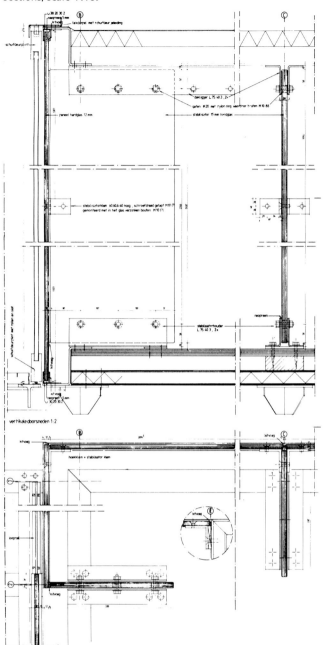

Plan, prior to adding the extension, scale 1:125.

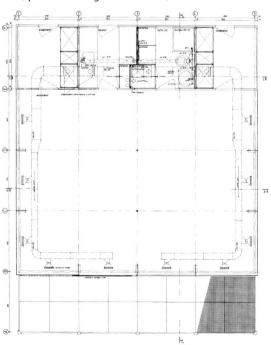

Private house, Almere
Benthem Crouwel

The design for this experimental glass house was awarded a prize in the 1982 "Unusual Living" competition sponsored by the "De Fantasie" foundation. The rules specified the use of a 20 x 20 m plot for a duration of five years, after which the building was to be dismantled without leaving any traces behind on the plot itself. The prizewinners were themselves able to pay for the implementation of their design. Therefore, the competition sponsors allowed a great degree of freedom. Besides the basic principles of structural stability and fire protection, no other building codes needed to be observed.

The plot of land was located on the Flevoland polder in the Ijsselmeer, 18 km east of Amsterdam. A foundation in this region would normally require concrete piles 15 m deep. However, the requirement to vacate the site without leaving any traces precluded this option. The design – which was put together between 5 a.m. and 4 p.m. on the day before the competition deadline! – aimed to provide a "minimum" house involving low capital outlay, low weights and a few, prefabricated, reusable components. The layout comprised a living room, two bedrooms, bathroom and kitchen, with the grid being based on the length of a bed, i.e. 2 m. This resulted in an open living room measuring 6 x 8 m and four separate rooms each 2 x 2 m – overall just 8 x 8 m for the complete house!

The separate rooms as well as the floor comprised sandwich panels of plywood and polyurethane foam, as used in refrigerated goods vehicles. The walls to the living room are 12 mm toughened safety glass, the butt joints between the individual panes being sealed with clear silicone. Together, the three glass walls and the sandwich panels carry the steel roof, which is secured against wind loads by two tension cables. The glass walls are stiffened by 15 mm glass stiffeners. To be able to use the glass as a structural member, it had to be guaranteed that the whole construction would not collapse if two adjacent panes were to fail. The snow load for the roof was taken as 50 kg/m^2 and the wind suction as 75 kg/m^2.

With all openings closed, this glass building heats up very rapidly; however, with adequate ventilation it also cools down again quickly owing to the low storage mass. Lightweight metal blinds were incorporated to provide shade and privacy. A warm-air heating system is used in the winter. The whole house stands on a pre-

Location
De Fantasie 10, Almere,
Netherlands

Client
Benthem Crouwel Architekten
BV, Amsterdam

Design
Benthem Crouwel

Date of completion
1984

Extended
1991

Sculpture pavilion in
Arnhem.

Section, prior to adding the
extension, scale 1:125.

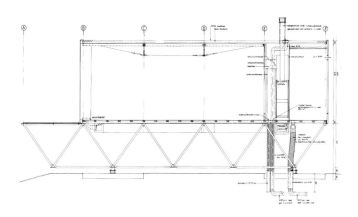

Plan, after adding the
extension, scale 1:125.

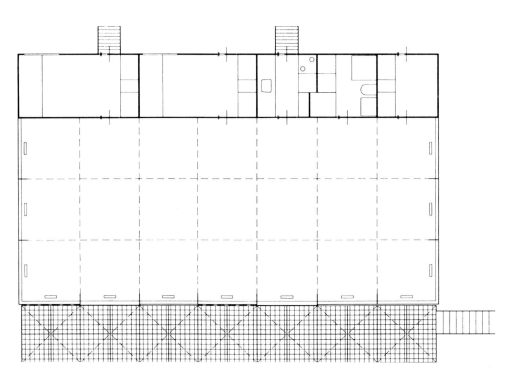

fabricated space frame placed on top of prefabricated industrial-quality concrete flooring slabs. The house built by the architects themselves in 1984 was extended by a further three bays in 1991 after the licence to use the plot was prolonged. It is the home of Jan Benthem and his family. Undoubtedly, living in such an experimental house does have its drawbacks. Nevertheless, Jan Benthem regards the structure as a laboratory in which he can gather impressions for his work and test materials and techniques.

One of the results of the experience gained in this way was the glass pavilion erected in 1986 for the sculpture exhibition in the park of the old Sonsbeek House in Arnhem. The theme of that exhibition was "The Skin", and a small-scale architectural competition was held to design pavilions for the open-air exhibits. The glass structure designed by Benthem Crouwel measured 24 x 6 x 3 m high. It utilized toughened safety glass, 10 mm thick for the walls, 15 mm for the glass stiffeners, and for the roof glazing laminated safety glass consisting of two 8 mm panes and a 2 mm PVB interlayer. The panes of laminated safety glass forming the roof span from yoke to yoke, 13 in total, formed by the glass stiffeners and a steel truss. The glass stiffeners are bolted to the truss and to the floor, and glued to the glass walls using silicone.

Both projects are early examples of modern structural glazing. While the pavilion for the sculpture exhibition was taken down after three months and not re-erected, the house in Almere remains inhabited to this day.

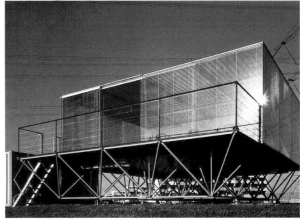

South elevation.

Steps to terrace at south-west corner.

Plan, upper level,
scale 1:1000.

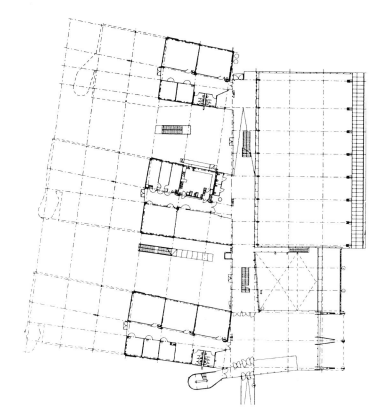

Plan, entrance level,
scale 1:1000.

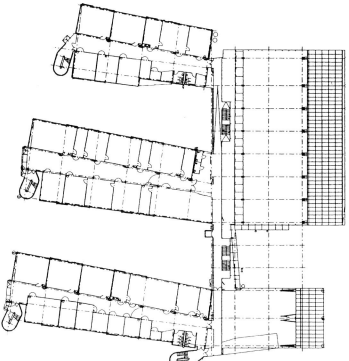

29

Combined secondary schools, Vienna
Helmut Richter

This building explores new paths in school design, both in terms of its conception and its construction. Transparency and maximum use of daylight are utilized in an economic and ecological manner, exploiting their physical and psychological effects. Situated on a confined site within a development of small units, adjacent to the Baumgartner Cemetery and a number of small shops selling flowers and gravestones, the school is the only large structure in the area. However, it lends the district a sort of "backbone", rather than acting as a disturbing factor. The clear, functional architecture, the large areas of reflective glazing, contrast and at the same time communicate with the heterogeneous environment in a self-confident manner, without needing to adapt in any way. Nevertheless, the building makes use of the south-facing slope, emphasizing the large monopitch glass roof which marks the southern end of the school; glass is the only material that can bring about such an interaction. The layout for 600 pupils, spread over 20 classes plus the five classes of the whole-day pilot scheme, actually comprises two schools: a secondary school with a normal (half-day) and a trial whole-day curriculum, and a computer science secondary school. The glazed entrance and recreation hall, the recreation yard and the 48-m-long triple sports hall, the floor of which is up to 7 m below ground level, on the southern side are joined to three wings to the north which enclose terraced inner courtyards set into the slope. The two outer wings house the classrooms for the two schools, while the centre wing accommodates common facilities: refectory, library, chemistry and crafts units. Each of the three wings has rooms arranged on both sides of a central corridor which gradually widens out like a cone towards the north, leading to freestanding escape stairs in fully glazed shafts. Another glazed escape stair is located adjacent the bridge which leads to the main entrance. From here, an internal corridor runs in a west-east direction from the entrance and recreation hall, which is up to 15 m high, past the recreation yard and along the side of the large sports hall. At ground floor level, this corridor is separated by a glass wall from the spectators' gallery overlooking the sports hall. The internal stairs and the upper galleries are finished off with inclined glazing on the sports hall side, thus allowing a view of the hall and of the outside too through the glass roof. Light, air and the clear, minimal structure create a feeling of openness.

Location
Doppelhauptschule Waidhausenstrasse,
1140 Vienna, Austria

Client
Vienna City Council

Architect
Prof. Helmut Richter, Vienna

Assistance
Jakob Dunkl, Gert Erhartt,
Andreas Gerner, Heide Mehring

Structural engineers
Vasko & Partner, Lothar
Heinrich, Vienna

Thermal consultant
Prof. Dr Erich Panzhauser,
Institute of Structural
Engineering for Architects,
Vienna Technical University

Glazing
Brüder Eckelt & Co., Steyr

Date of completion
1994

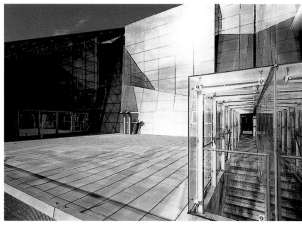

The inner access block has
inclined glazing on the
sports hall side.

Inner courtyard with view
looking towards stairs in the
sports hall.

Detail of monopitch glass
roof over recreation yard.

View towards recreation yard and glass roofs. On the left, the entrance hall; on the right, the sports hall.

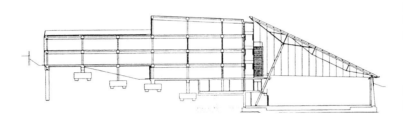

Section through triple sports hall, scale 1:1000.

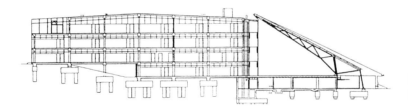

Section through recreation hall, scale 1:1000.

Materials and air-conditioning

The patented "Litewall" system of individual bolted fixings was employed for the fully glazed walls and the inclined roof glazing. Together with the minimal main structure, this resulted in an extraordinarily transparent solution. Design work was preceded by studies carried out by Prof. Dr Erich Panzhauser as to the thermal load in summer, particularly for the sports hall, under the 1550 m^2 of the extensive glazed roof. The outcome was an insulating glass construction with an outer pane of green solar-control, toughened safety glass, 8 mm thick, a cavity of 12 mm and an inner pane of laminated safety glass, 16 mm thick, the inside of which is printed with a pattern of white dots with a coverage density of 30%. This glazing system has a total energy transmittance value (g) of 21% and a U value of 1.8 W/m^{2}K. Prof. Dr Panzhauser explains: "The glazing system I have outlined, tailored to cope with the conditions encountered, in conjunction with an internal, highly reflective screen with a silk-paint finish means that at the height of the summer the thermal loading which can be expected in the hall is reduced to such an extent that a pleasant, internal summer climate can be guaranteed in the sports hall." Besides the natural ventilation by means of vents near the eaves and near the ridge, mechanical back-up ventilation with a fresh-air temperature of 18°C on hot summer days and un-conditioned outside air at night ensures that the temperature during hot summer

Detail of inclined glazing made from insulating glass over recreation yard showing the individual bolted fixings of the "Litewall-Iso-System".

Recreation hall looking towards covered car parking area.

The triple sports hall under the extensive glass roof, view of gable wall. On the left, the open spectators' stand; above, the rising wall of inclined glazing separating the hall from the access block.

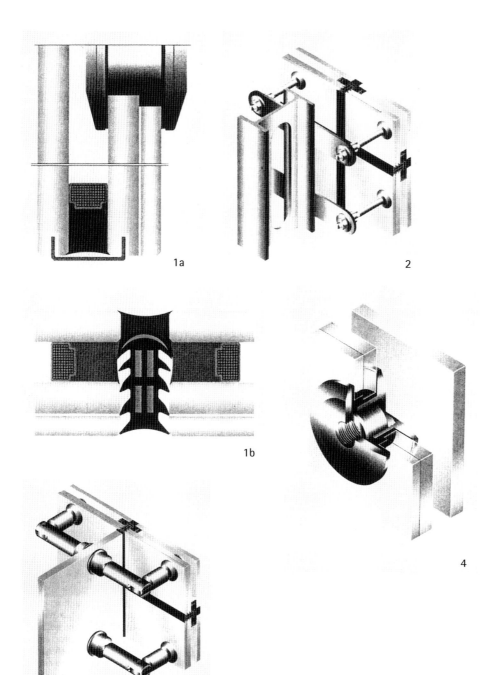

Details of "Litewall-Iso-System":

1a Vertical section through insulating glass unit; the bolted fixing only affects the inner pane. 1b Horizontal section through joint between two insulating glass units. 2 Individual fixings on threaded bars. 3 Articulated arm on glass stiffener construction. 4 "Litewall-Iso" fitting. The insulating glass units are fastened to the inner panes by means of individual bolted fixings, which avoids creating a thermal transmission at the point of fixing. The outside surface is not penetrated and so forms a smooth skin. The patented fixings are made from stainless steel.

1a

2

1b

3

4

periods does not rise above 27°C in the playing areas of the sports hall. This result was due to the cooperation between architect, thermal consultant and a glass manufacturer eager to explore new ideas. The new "Litewall-Iso-System" which originated from this collaboration comprises a double-glazing, thermally separate, insulating glass design with the individual bolted fixings attached to the inner pane so that no thermal transmission can occur at the fixing positions. At the same time, this principle allows all functions, such as thermal protection and shading, to be transferred to the intact outer pane. The patented austenitic stainless steel fixings are pre-installed in the pane of insulating glass at the works, providing a flexible seal but protecting against vapour diffusion. They are capable of accommodating static and dynamic forces and transferring them to the supporting structure. An Austrian technical licence for the "Litewall-Iso-System" has been applied for.

Section, landside–airside,
scale 1:2500.

Site plan, scale approx.
1:15 000.

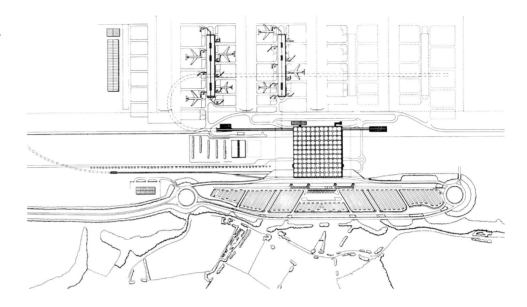

34

Plan of arrivals/departures
level, scale 1:2500.

1 Departures concourse.
2 Check-in area. 3 Security
and passport control.
4 Departure lounge. 5 Shops.
6 Catering. 7 Domestic
channel. 8 Immigration
control, arrivals. 9 Baggage
reclaim hall. 10 Customs.
11 Arrivals concourse.
12 Management offices.
13 Drop-off point for buses
and taxis. 14 Track transit
platforms. 15 Airside bus
terminals. 16 Track transit
system.

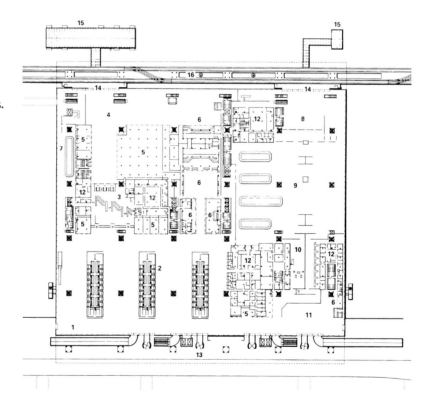

Forecourt. The fully glazed
entrance elevation is
situated 18 m back from the
front edge of the canopy.

35

Airport terminal Stansted, London
Sir Norman Foster

To relieve London's two major international airports at Heathrow and Gatwick, a
third airport was established on the site of a former military airfield at Stansted.
The British Airports Authority (now BAA plc) appointed the architects to carry out
preliminary studies as far back as 1981. The new terminal was to be cheaper than
previous BAA terminals, more convenient for passengers and remain flexible for
future developments. One further criterion was that the building should not disturb
the gently undulating Essex countryside around the airport. Sir Norman Foster,
architect und private pilot, based his concept for the new terminal on the early days
of aviation, when passengers still walked across the tarmac from the hangar to the
aircraft. He wanted to avoid the seemingly endless trek through halls, long corri-
dors and flights of stairs so customary these days, where the passenger only
glimpses sight of the aircraft at the very end. He has accomplished this wish with
his design.

    Stansted Airport lies about 52 km north of the centre of London and has good
links with the road network. British Rail's *Stansted Express* takes about 40 minutes
from Liverpool Street Station in the heart of London to the airport. The Airport is
designed for eight million passengers annually, although there is scope to extend it
to handle 11 million. Work on the access roads commenced in 1986 and, shortly
after, the building itself. The terminal was inaugurated in 1991.

Design

The complex takes advantage of an undulation in the site, the main hall being constructed at the crown of this rise. On the landside, access is at the same level, in
front of the hall. The short-stay parking area as well as the bus terminal are situated to the south at a lower level, with access to the building beneath the forecourt. Also below the forecourt, at basement level, is the railway station for the
Stansted Express. Ramps and lifts ensure easy access to the hall, which accommodates both arrivals and departures on one level. Apart from the railway station, the
basement houses all technical services, stores and baggage handling. No services
are located on the roof, thus permitting a simple, unconstrained design. The whole
complex is conceived in such a way that contact with daylight is maintained in all

Location
Stansted Airport, Essex, UK

Client
British Airports Authority (now
BAA plc), London

Architects
Sir Norman Foster & Partners,
London
Sir Norman Foster and
Spencer de Grey

Project manager
John Silver

Assistance
Arthur Branthwaite,
Chris Eisner, Katy Harris,
Paul Kalkofen, Alex Reid,
Winston Shu, Kohn Small,
Chris Windsor

Structural engineers
Ove Arup & Partners, London

Lighting design
Claude and Danielle Engle,
Washington DC

Glazing
Brüder Eckelt & Co., Steyr,
Austria

Date of completion
1991

Schematic drawing of
overhead lighting.

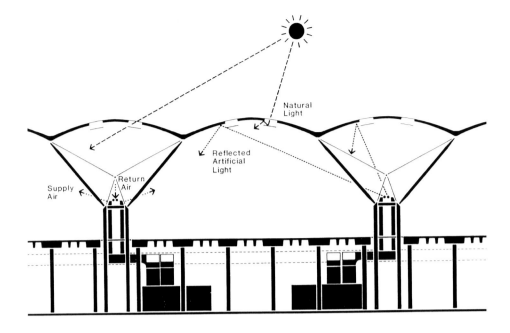

36

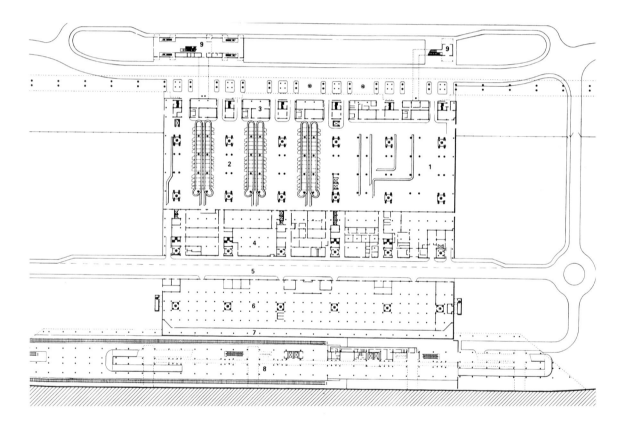

Plan of ground floor,
scale 1:2500.

1 Baggage handling, arrivals.
2 Baggage handling, departures. 3 Airside operations
offices. 4 Duty-free, customs
and general storage.
5 Service road. 6 Plant hall.
7 Fresh air supply duct.
8 British Rail station.
9 Airside bus terminals.

areas and the unobstructed views make signposting almost superfluous. The glazed areas make valuable contributions in these respects.

Construction

The columns and roof were erected first. This enabled the concrete for the basement to be cast while protected from the weather. The roof structure consists of 121 dome elements, each 18 x 18 m, covering a square area measuring 198 x 198 m. The hall itself is 198 m wide by 162 m deep and the roof cantilevers 18 m beyond the building on both landside and airside. Thirty-six freestanding "tree-like" column structures arranged on a 36 x 36 m grid are used to support the roof. This grid spacing was chosen to suit the functional requirements of the terminal, particularly with respect to the space necessary for passenger handling. The tree-like structures consist of four 458-mm-diameter hollow steel sections arranged at the corners of a square, 3 x 3 m, which extend the 12 m from the foundation to the point at which they "branch out". These "branches" begin 4 m above hall floor level and extend upwards at 45° to form a square of 18 x 18 m at their upper ends where they carry the dome elements at a height of 15 m above the floor. The eaves are at a height of 12 m and so the overall height of the building roughly corresponds with the height of mature trees in the vicinity. To provide natural lighting in the hall, each dome includes four triangular glass bays of insulating glass (2 panes of 6 mm toughened safety glass, low-emissivity coating, gas-filled), a total of 11 m^2 per dome. Perforated metal "sails" suspended below these non-coloured, transparent rooflights allow light to enter at a shallow angle. However, sunlight directly from above is filtered by the sails and reflected back up to the underside of the roof. At night, the domes are lit from below by specially designed halogen metal vapour floodlights fitted to the columns.

Rooflights of non-slip, printed, laminated safety glass capable of taking pedestrian traffic.

The glass-covered ramp between the levels. Frameless glass construction with Eckelt "Litewall" system of individual bolted fixings.

The walls separating the incoming and outgoing controls are printed with a pattern of white dots to make them semi-transparent.

International departures

Please have your boarding card ready for inspection

Only one piece of hand baggage per person is allowed in the aircraft cabin

All items of baggage are subject to x-ray

Baggage must not be left unattended

No smoking

No trolleys

No postal facilities beyond this point

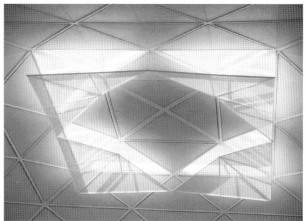

Departures concourse and check-in area. The roof is supported by 36 freestanding "tree-like" structures. Daylight penetrates into the hall via rooflights.

Perforated metal "sails" below the rooflights allow light to enter at a shallow angle. However, sunlight directly from above is filtered by the sails and reflected back up to the underside of the roof.

Detail of roof/wall junction. Insulating glass with antiglare interlayer in upper section.

Glazing

Some 3% of the total area of the roof is glazed. This guarantees a light intensity of 180 lux on a clear winter's day. Generally, in terms of overall brightness and glare, the lighting concept had to take account of the computer screens on the counters. The external walls of the hall are fully glazed; the north and south walls below the cantilevered roof are transparent in their full height, while the upper two-thirds of those on the east and west ends are translucent, achieved by laminated safety glass with a translucent PVB interlayer. This prevents glare and the transmission of solar radiation. All glazing units are made from "Climaplus" insulating glass and measure 3.60 x 1.83 m. The U value of this glass is approx. 1.0 W/m²K. The glass wall with thermally separate aluminium sections has a total U value of 1.6 W/m²K. Safety regulations prevented the architects from fully implementing their plan of a see-through terminal building, with a view right through from entrance to runway. Passenger handling and departure area as well as baggage reclaim, customs and the exit are all separated by a translucent glass wall covered with a pattern of white dots. The glazed ramps which lead up from the *Stansted Express* railway station into the hall are provided with glass roofs. The frameless construction uses the Eckelt "Litewall" system of individual bolted fixings to hold the glass in place. The flat roof glazing consists of laminated safety glass. The vertical glazing is toughened safety glass, 10 mm thick. Rooflights of non-slip, printed, laminated safety glass capable of taking pedestrian traffic are positioned flush with the floor in the vicinity of the tree structures in front of the entrance to allow daylight to penetrate into the basement. The restaurant area is decorated with the glass paintings of Brian Clark.

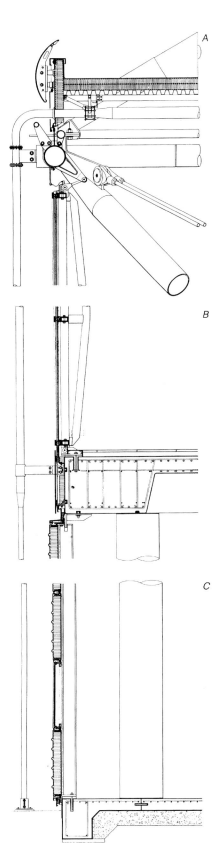

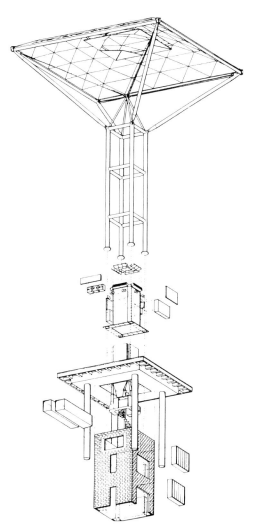

Exploded view of "tree" structure with stairs down to lower level.

Details of façade.

A) Detail of junction between roof and east/west wall. "Climaplus" insulating glass with antiglare interlayer in upper section.

B) At hall floor level. "Climaplus" insulating glass, transparent.

C) At basement level. Aluminium sandwich panels. "Climaplus" insulating glass with antiglare interlayer.

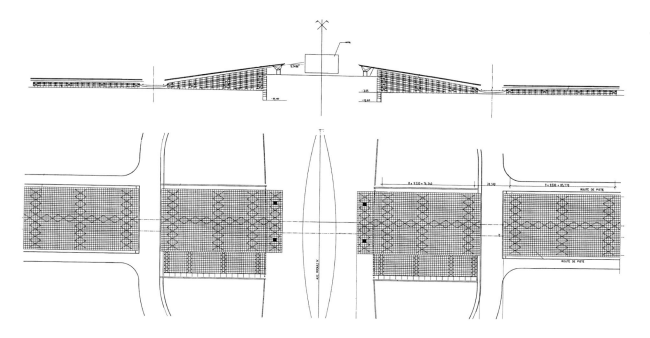

40

Elevation and plan of the
four glass roofs,
scale approx. 1:3000.

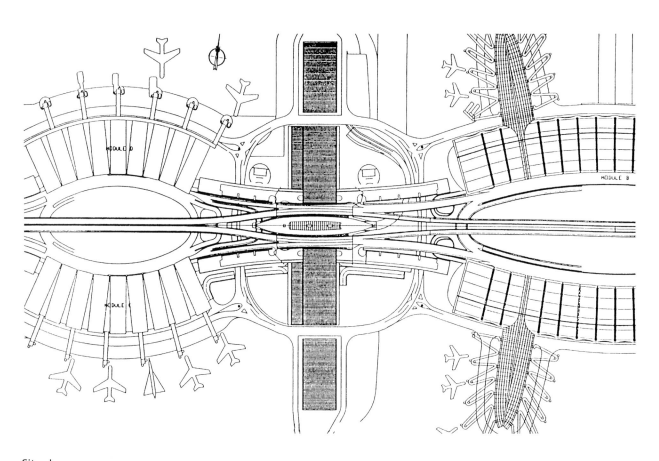

Site plan.

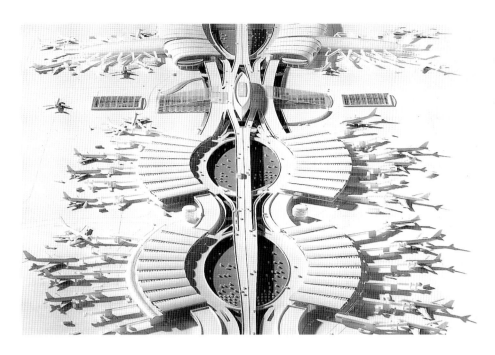

Model of the complete
Roissy–Charles de Gaulle
airport. The TGV station with
its four enormous glass roofs
passes between terminals 1
and 2.

41

TGV railway station, Roissy–CDG airport, Paris
Paul Andreu

Twenty years after its opening in 1974, the large Roissy-Charles de Gaulle airport in Paris was augmented with a station to provide a direct link to the high-speed TGV rail network. Officially, the station is designated "module d'échanges", which roughly means "interchange module". This is a transportation interface; aircraft, inter-city and regional trains, the airport rail shuttle, buses, taxis and private cars all meet here. The Roissy-CDG TGV station is not only conceived as a station serving the airport; on the contrary, it fulfils all the requirements of another station serving Paris, situated on the new high-speed line which since 1994 skirts the city's eastern suburbs. The journey to and from Paris with the suburban passenger train service RER (Réseau Express Regional) takes a little over 30 minutes. It is assumed that by 1998 about 40% of the two million railway passengers expected to use the station will not be on their way to the airport but rather Paris and the northern part of the Ile de France. A total of 25 million passengers pass through the airport itself each year and for more than 100 million European citizens it is less than three hours to Roissy-CDG airport by high-speed TGV train! The TGVs are not seen as a rival by airport operator Aéroports de Paris but instead as a welcome partner, relieving the load on short-haul flights and bringing customers to the airport.

The new railway station extends in a north-south direction between the terminals. It serves five different types of transport. The two TGV platforms and single RER platform are situated on level 1 at third basement level; two tracks in the centre allow the passage of TGV through-trains. Above, level 2 houses the SNCF service centre with ticket sales, information, waiting rooms, shops and offices. The driverless, fully automatic airport rail shuttle runs on level 3 to link the airport terminals with the railway station. The arcade-like pedestrian concourse through which most travellers have to pass is also on this level. A floor of translucent concrete blocks illuminated from below serves to emphasize the significance of this thoroughfare. At ground floor level, passageways provide links to the departure halls. This level also has parking for 15,800 vehicles, 800 spaces being reserved exclusively for rail passengers. A ramp enables buses and taxis to reach the first floor. The long cantilever of the glass roof over the TGV hall, which is connected to all other levels by way of lifts, offers travellers protection from the weather.

Location
Roissy-Charles de Gaulle
airport, Paris-Roissy, France

Client
Aéroports de Paris
SNCF, Département de
bâtiments, Paris

Architect
Paul Andreu, Paris, with
Aéroports de Paris

Project Manager
Anne Brisson
SNCF: Jean-Marie Duthilleul,
Michael Maillard, Etienne
Tricaud with Agence d'études
des gares de la SNCF

Project Manager
Daniel Claris

Structural design
Peter Rice with
Rice-Francis-Ritchie

Project Manager
Hugh Dutton

Roof design
Ove Arup and
Rice-Francis-Ritchie

Lighting design
Light Cible, Louis Clair

Glass construction
Helmut Fischer GmbH, Talheim

Date of completion
1994

Looking towards the TGV platforms.

Individual bolted fixings for the panes of the fully glazed façade to the station hall.

View from the pedestrian concourse towards the TGV platforms.

Fully glazed façade on pitched glass roof with transition to shed–type roof over the tracks of the RER suburban railway.

The pitched glass roof is supported on a primary construction made from arc-shaped steel girders with prestressed members above carrying the compression to lateral spring/strut assemblies while the tension is taken below.

43

Glass roofs and façades

The design was realized by a consortium of companies. A British company undertook the design of the primary supporting structure and a German firm the glass construction. The technical and logistics requirements of the four large glass roofs and the glass façades of the station placed exceedingly high demands on these companies. This resulted in the kind of precision work normally only found in mechanical engineering. In order to avoid impairing the transparency of the roof glazing more than necessary, the arc-shaped steel roof girders were provided with prestressed members above carrying the compression via lateral spring/strut assemblies, while the tension is taken below. The structural calculations for the entire glass construction were undertaken by the German company. The steel tonnage was able to be reduced by 10% with respect to the original estimate.

The entire area of the roof was modelled mathematically in the calculations and 450 working drawings were produced to enable accurate assembly. The roofs are glazed with toughened safety glass, 8 mm thick, each pane measuring 1590 x 1490 mm. Overhead single glazing is not permitted in Germany as such panes have no residual strength upon breakage and the splinters of glass fall without warning. In contrast, laminated safety glass with its viscoplastic PVB interlayer has sufficient residual strength to prevent pieces of glass dropping down immediately upon breakage. A test was necessary in France to gain approval for the use of toughened safety glass. This proved that the panes by far exceeded the required values for pressure and suction loadings. TGV trains passing through the station at speeds of up to 170 km/h also had to be considered in these calculations.

To guarantee glare-free and even daylight, the panes of the roof glazing were printed with a light-blue striped pattern which makes the sky appear friendly even when overcast! The striped pattern was employed in four grades: 20, 40, 60 and 80% transparency, distributed according to lighting requirements. The striped pattern was applied using ceramic inks in a silk-screen printing process. The printing was then baked on in a furnace which simultaneously served to prestress the panes to create safety glass. The printing is weatherproof and resistant to ultra-violet radiation. To simplify erection, each container of glass for the flat roofs contained 17 panes in the correct order according to position and degree of transparency; two containers were required for the 34 panes of each of the transverse rows. Each pane was held in place by eight "patch" fittings (uplift anchors). The butt joints

Details of glass construction

Flat roofs
4,323 panes = 9,500 m²

Pitched roofs
4,508 panes = 10,500 m²

RER roof (shed-type roof):
1,738 panes = 2,800 m²

Glass façades
1,538 panes = 5,970 m²

Silicone sealant
8,000 cartridges = 30 km

"Patch" fixings
60,000 pieces

Steel
415 t

between panes are sealed with silicone. While only six different types of pane were required for the two flat roofs, the two pitched glass roofs needed 88! On top of that, rainwater gutters are necessary on the pitched glass roofs. These gutters were formed by including transparent glass upstands, 200 mm high. The loading case for the anticipated volume of rainwater and its velocity were simulated and calculated. Robots are used for cleaning the outside of this vast expanse of glass and for maintenance. These robots traverse the roof construction on trestles mounted in the roof structure at a regular spacing. The glass façades are made from toughened safety glass, 12 mm thick, held in place by individual bolted fixings.

44

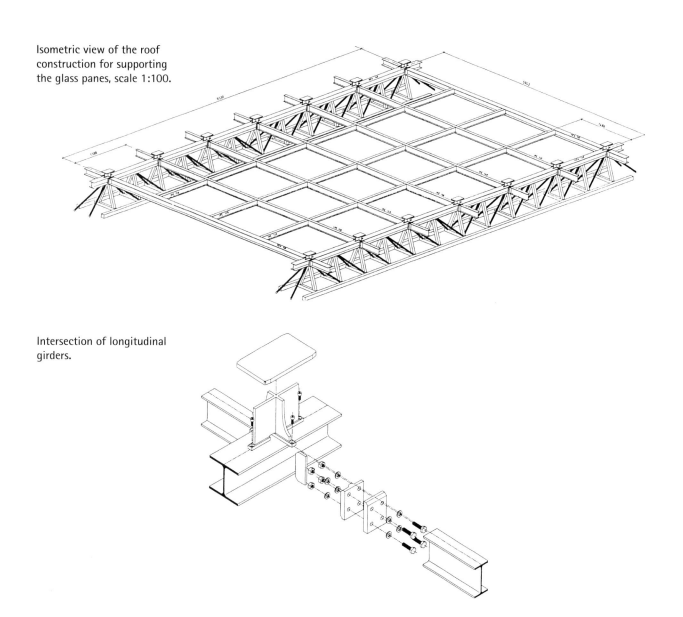

Isometric view of the roof construction for supporting the glass panes, scale 1:100.

Intersection of longitudinal girders.

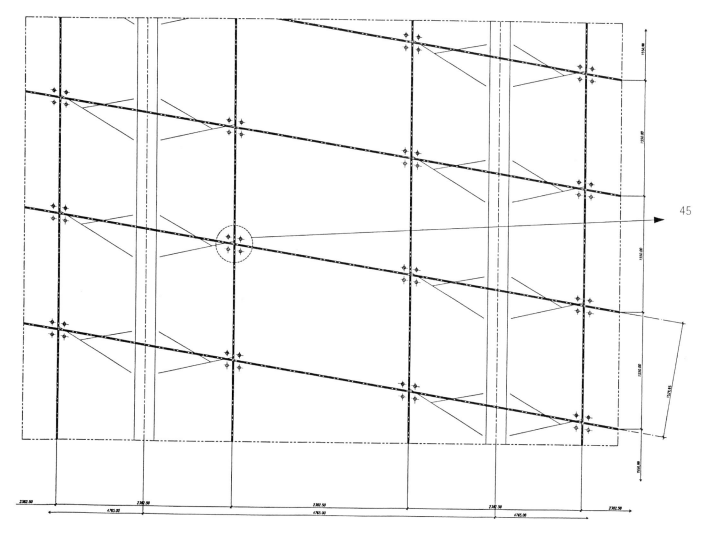

45

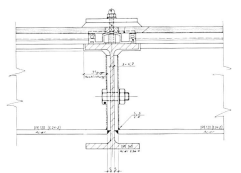

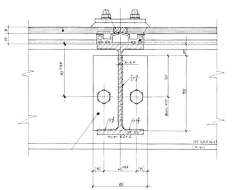

Individual bolted fixings
for the panes of the glass
curtain wall to the station
hall, scale 1:50.

Details of roof glazing,
scale 1:5.

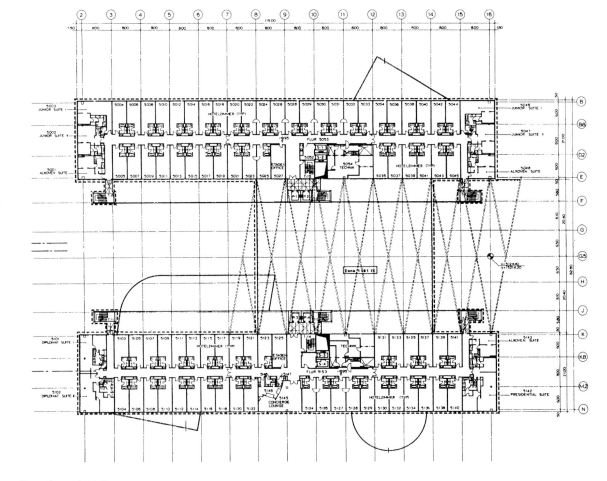

Plan of standard floor,
scale 1:1000.

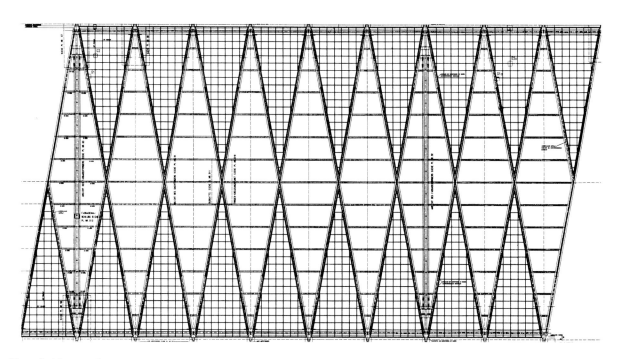

Plan of atrium roof,
scale 1:500.

Entrance elevation. The 40 x 25 m glass façade of the atrium has a supporting structure made up of pretensioned steel cables. The calculated deformation is approx. 900 mm at the centre of the façade. The block-type, 24 m high, 21 m wide and 113 m long hotel wings have storey-height façade elements with acoustic insulation glazing (acoustic insulation value 54 dB). The glass is silk-screen printed "Litex-Design", transparent and opaque.

Hotel Kempinski, Munich Airport
Murphy/Jahn

This new hotel serving Munich Airport makes very impressive use of glass both internally and externally. Two hotel blocks, each 113 m long, 21 m wide and 24 m high, flank a large inner courtyard. The area of the inner courtyard between transverse grid lines 8-17 and longitudinal grid lines E-K offers a floor area uninterrupted by columns and is spanned by a glass roof. At both ends, at transverse grid lines 8 and 14, full-height, extraordinarily transparent glass curtain walls close off the atrium – 48 m long x 40 m wide x 29.5 m high to the apex. The façades of the two hotel wings are also made completely of glass – but opaque apart from the window areas. Glass walls, high glass shelving and glass stairs are dominant features of the interior design.

Glass lattice façade

The 40 x 25 m transparent glass façade of the entrance elevation is supported by pretensioned steel cables spanning between specially braced structures on both sides. The crossing horizontal and vertical cables are prestressed in such a way that they can transfer wind loads perpendicular to the plane of the lattice to the two structures at the sides. The horizontal cables are more highly prestressed than the vertical ones because, in addition to wind, these also have to carry the dead load of the cable system and the panes of glass.

At roof level, the vertical cables are attached to an arched beam with a tie consisting of several 46-mm-diameter cables to prevent deformation. The façade beam is similar in section to the roof beams and is connected to the latter at the support so that a joint loadbearing effect is achieved.

At their intersections, the cables of the façade lattice are joined together with clamps specially developed for this purpose. These cast stainless steel clamps are shaped in such a way that they also serve as supports for the panes of glass. The spacing of the cables (1.5 x 1.5 m) was determined by the load of the glass panes (individual fixings). Such a support system – a taut net in one plane – can only absorb loads acting perpendicular to that plane by deforming – if the forces are stronger than the rigid façade construction. The calculated deformation of the façade, designed for wind loads according to DIN 1055/4, is approx. 900 mm in the

Location
Munich Airport, near
85435 Erding, Germany

Client
Flughafen München GmbH

Architects
Murphy/Jahn, Chicago

Structural engineers
Schlaich, Bergermann &
Partner, Stuttgart

Assistance
Karl Friedrich, Peter Schulze

Roof and glass lattice walls
Helmut Fischer GmbH, Talheim

Glass façades
Josef Gartner & Co.,
Gundelfingen

"Litex-Design" silk-screen
printed glass
Brüder Eckelt & Co., Steyr,
Austria

Date of completion
1995

Partly glazed escape stair tower.

The façades of the hotel wings are glazed in a square pattern. Glass elements in front of solid structural members are toughened safety glass with two-coat, blue and white, special silk-screen printing. The insulating glass elements of the windows have a wide-mesh, white-dot pattern.

The roof spans over the 40 m wide and 48 m long atrium which is closed off by the two glass lattice-structure walls. Roof glazing of printed, laminated safety glass, 10 mm thick. All-glass shelving units with artificial geraniums and palm trees decorate the atrium.

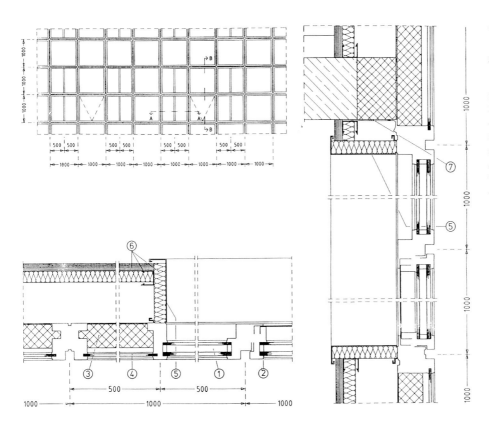

Glass façade of hotel wings. Elevation, vertical and horizontal detail section.

1 Sound-absorbing, double-glazed, solar-control units. 2 Neoprene. 3 Steel panel. 4 Toughened safety glass, 8 mm thick. 5 Aluminium connection profile. 6 Spandrel and column cladding. 7 Sheet steel connection trims, 3 mm thick.

centre. However, the windspeeds on which the calculations are based are extremely unlikely to occur here, given the local circumstances. The anchors for the cables are designed to cope with larger deformations if necessary.

The cables are prestressed by means of special tensioning devices anchored in the structural concrete of the side walls and floor slab of level +5.20 m. This prestressing is carried out in a controlled manner, i.e. according to the defined paths of the prestressing forces, the elongation. The amount of prestress in the structure can be readjusted at any time, but this is not normally necessary.

The glazing comprises laminated safety glass, 10 mm thick. The mountings for the individual panes of glass, 1.5 x 1.5 m, at the node points of the lattice are fully floating so that the glazing can deform with the structure. Trials were carried out on full-size assemblies to determine the deformability of the panes in their mountings.

The cables which are omitted to allow for the entrance doors are replaced by a frame construction made from steel sections. This frame has a pin-jointed base so that it too can follow the deformations of the lattice. The amount of prestress in the anchoring can be readjusted at any time.

The following materials have been used:
Lattice cables: stainless steel, 22 mm diameter
End fittings: threaded stainless steel fittings
Node connections: cast stainless steel
Ties for arched beams: fully locked spiral cables with galvanized wires
Façade beams: welded box-section beams as required, St 37/St 52 steel
Glass: laminated safety glass, 10 mm thick

Roof structure

The roof structure consists of individual box-section arched beams which are all supported on the edges of the roofs to the hotel wings. They each span about 40 m diagonally across the bay width of 8 m. This means that each pair of arched beams crosses in the centre of a bay, where a tie rod and vertical compression member

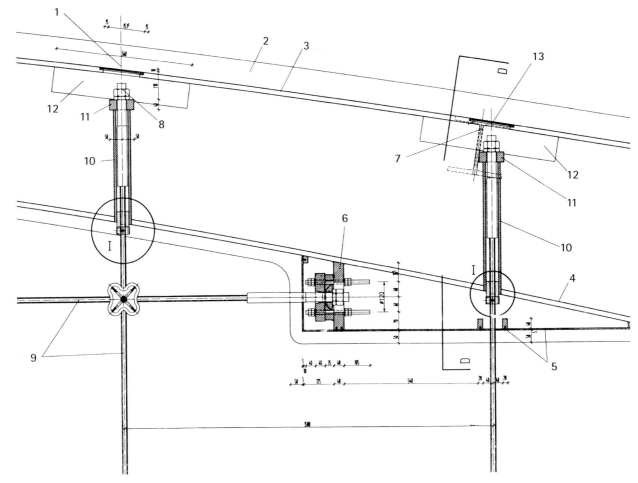

Detail of upper cable lattice connections, scale 1:15.

1 Closing plate, 180 x 146 x 5 mm, with soft-rubber strips glued to top chord plate fastened with M6 countersunk head screws (DIN 963). 2 Profiled roof sheeting, 100 x 1 mm.
3 Top chord, 500 x 20 mm.
4 Bottom chord, 260 x 20 mm. 5 Cover plates, 268 x 5 mm, with welded U-shaped glass mounting attached with M6 countersunk head screws (DIN 963) to fixing lugs, 40 x 20 mm.
6 Transverse element, 260 x 40 mm, with hole, 120 mm ø. 7 Stiffener, 175 x 200 x 20 mm, for connecting roof beam. 8 Threaded fitting, 410 mm long, M36 hexagonal nut (DIN 934) and M36 locknut (DIN 936).
9 Stainless steel cable, 22 mm ø, spiral cable, 1 x 19 mm. 10 Steel tube, ø 70 x 10 mm. 11 Bearing plate, 100 x 80 x 40 mm, with central hole, 40 mm ø.
12 Stiffener, 560 x 100 x 10 mm, both sides of assembly hole. 13 Closing plate, 180 x 146 x 5 mm.

Lower cable lattice connection, scale 1:15.

1 Tensioning plate, 210 x 190 x 40 mm, with countersunk hole, ø 65/52 L=32, and recess, ø 106 x 2 mm and 4 No. holes, 26 mm ø.
2 Oval tube, ø 114.3 x 2.6 mm, with welded fixing plate, 130 x 150 x 4 mm, with 4 No. hexagon-head screws, M6 x 15.
3 Laminated safety glass
4 U-shaped glass mounting, glass fixing with seal.
5 Insert made from sheet metal, 240 x 220 x 15 mm, with central hole, 120 mm ø, and neoprene strips glued on, welded tube, ø 127 x 3 mm, and 4 No. M16 anchor bars, grade 10.9.
6 Frame made from sheet metal, 70 x 15 mm mit 4 No. holes, ø 17 mm.

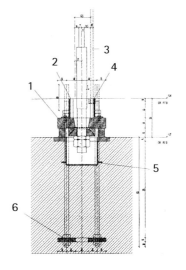

provide extra stability. These pairs of beams are supported on continuous girders of circular hollow sections along the sides of the hotel wings; these girders project beyond the façade where they also serve to support the arched beams. Nibs on the reinforced concrete building carry the girders on the main grid lines. The connections are real pins in order to avoid secondary forces from the movements of roof and building.

In order to stabilize the entire roof against lateral wind loads, short, additional ties or, alternatively, struts, are necessary between arched beams and nib supports. The intersections of the arched beams give rise to gusset-shaped roof areas which are partly glazed, partly filled with profiled roof sheeting.

The roof is made up as follows:
— transverse beams at approx. 3.0 m centres between arched beams,
— thermal insulation and flat metal roofing (with welted joints).
In the glazed areas:
— rigid, welded rectangular hollow sections on a 1 x 1 m grid,
— laminated safety glass infills, 10 mm thick, according to the "structural glazing" principle, i.e. with glued joints; the individual panes are secured against uplift due to wind suction by means of individual "patch" fittings; a pattern is printed on the glass for solar-control and antiglare purposes.

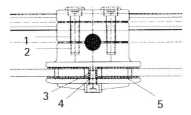

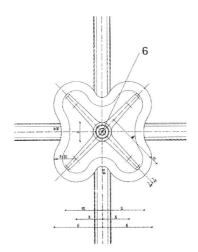

Cast stainless steel connection in cable lattice façade.

Cast stainless steel cable clamp for accommodating cable and fully floating mounting of laminated safety glass panes, scale 1:5.

1 Hole, 13 mm dia.
2 Threaded blind hole, M12.
3 Threaded blind hole, M10.
4 Hole, 11 mm dia. 5 Recess, 1 mm. 6 Set screw with hexagon-socket head, M10 x 20 mm (DIN 912).

Structural behaviour of the glass roof

The curvature of the roof about one axis and the supporting members connected rigidly with each other leads to a shell-shaped, grillage-type structure. Therefore, additional beams can be omitted in this area and the glazing bars utilized as loadbearing members. The deformations resulting from snow and self-weight are negligible in terms of the individual 1 x 1 m panes and the existing curvature of the roof. However, the cross-sections of the lattice supports have been arrived at in such a way that an adequate serviceability safety factor is guaranteed. The "shell" of the roof is bounded by a rigid edge section.

Glass stairs

Trussed glass stairs lead from the atrium down to the basement. The treads, 2.62 m wide, and the glass plates of the landing consist of non-slip, printed, laminated safety glass and were originally intended to be 33 mm thick. The characteristic permissible tensile bending strength had been taken as 30 N/mm^2 but at least 120 N/mm^2 was required for the ultimate bending strength. Therefore, the building authorities asked for a design incorporating 57-mm-thick laminated safety glass before they would give their approval.

Trussed glass stairs leading from the atrium down to the basement. The treads, 2.62 m wide, and the glass plates of the landing consist of non-slip, printed, laminated safety glass, 57 mm thick. A minimum value of 120 N/mm^2 was specified for the ultimate bending strength.

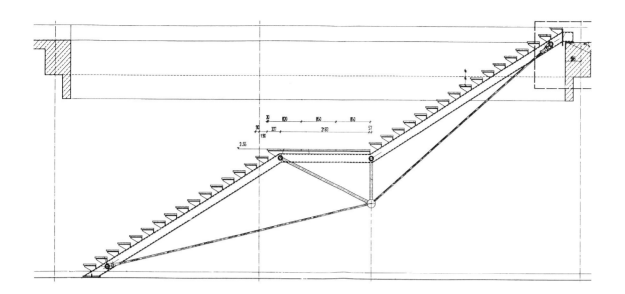

Longitudinal section.

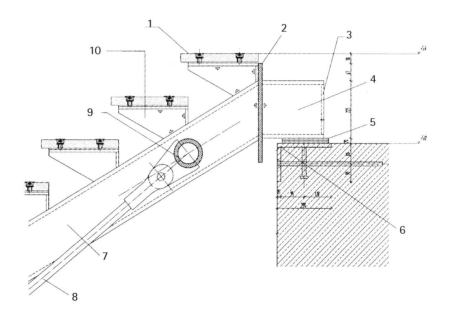

Detail of glass treads,
scale 1:15.

1 Tread, laminated safety
glass, 57 mm thick. 2 End
plate, 387 x 15 x 2640 mm.
3 Stiffeners, 2 No. 95 x 170
x 10 mm. 4 Cantilever beam
made from 2 No. HE–B 200,
225 mm deep, with welded
web plate, 25 x 10 x
250 mm, and 2 No. side
plates, 225 x 250 x 5 mm.
5 Bearing plate, 230 x
190 mm. 6 Welded angle
section made from 220 x 15
mm and 135 x 15 mm

plates, with 2 No. anchor
bars, 16 mm ø mild steel and
2 No. concrete anchors .
7 Stair stringer, HE–B 200,
with 2 No. welded side
plates, 200 x 5 mm. 8 Rod
anchor, 36 mm ø. 9 Circular
hollow section, ø 114.3 x
17.5 mm, with welded eye
plate, T=30, with hole,
31 mm ø. 10 Stair tread
support: horizontal plate,
100 x 10 x 280 mm, vertical
plate, 100 x 10 x 270 mm,
end stiffener, 100 x 10 mm.

Longitudinal section,
scale 1:200.

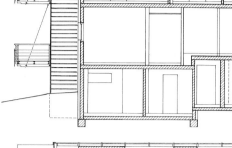

54

Plan, 1st floor,
scale 1:200.

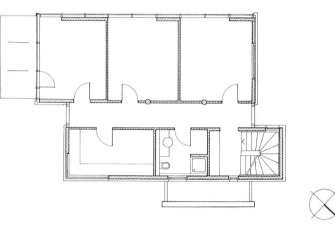

Plan, ground floor,
scale 1:200.

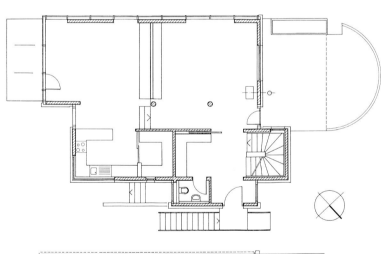

Plan, basement,
scale 1:200.

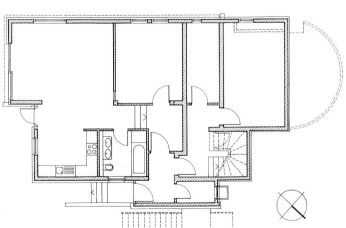

55

Low–energy house, Stuttgart
Hans–Ulrich Kilian

The design of this house was seen in engineering terms right from the outset. Plans and sections, structural calculations, heating and solar-energy technology were all fed into a computer simulation to achieve a complete 12-month dynamic energy balance, based on a reference year. The daylight ratios for the living area were also analysed by computer simulation. All in all, a considerable design effort out of all proportion to the size of the project. However, the designers were concerned here with a pilot scheme, obtaining fundamental experience on the way to low-energy housing.

The location of the building plot offered good prospects. The sloping site, just 14 m wide, faces south-east at the end of a small wooded valley. To the south-west, the plot is bounded by gardens on land not zoned for building. Therefore, optimum orientation towards the sun was possible. The architect explains the aim of the design: "Right from the start the intention was to design a low-energy house which, with justifiable expenditure, would need as little heating energy as possible. The use of solar gains and thermal insulation in conjunction with optimized services became our design brief. Furthermore, slender building components were to be favoured to achieve minimum use of – durable, mainly recyclable – materials. The objective was to develop an architectural form which matched the specification."

Utilization concept

The building at present comprises a main apartment, with rooms at ground floor, first floor and attic levels, and a second, self-contained apartment in the basement. Both apartments have separate access from outside but an internal staircase links all floors so that internal communication between both apartments is also possible. All floors incorporate cut-outs for the insertion of stairs to enable the building to be split up differently at a later date, e.g. basement + ground floor and first floor + attic, or ground floor + first floor with basement and attic separate. All floors can also be reached separately via the main stairs. If the layout is changed, then the inclusion of kitchens and bathrooms does not mean major conversion work but just simple additions. All living rooms face south-west. Kitchens, bathrooms and main stairs are housed in a self-contained section on the north-east side.

Location
Lindpaintnerstrasse 66,
70195 Stuttgart-Botnang,
Germany

Client
Hans-Ulrich Kilian

Architects
Kilian & Hagmann, Stuttgart
Prof. H.-U. Kilian, Mechthild
Deitermann

Structural engineers
Ingenieurbüro Dr Trompert,
Stuttgart

Building services
Ingenieurbüro Scheer, Stuttgart

Thermal and lighting
simulation
Fraunhofer Institute for Solar
Energy Systems, Freiburg
Dr M. Goller, S. Henkel

Transparent thermal insulation
Okalux Kapillarglas GmbH,
Marktheidenfeld-Altfeld

Date of completion
1995

Three-ply laminated safety glass, 34 mm thick, with a non-slip, ceramic ink coating, forms the floors to the balconies.

Window and transparent thermal insulation elements with blinds open.

South-east side. Balconies with glass floors.

Construction and technology

The massive core of the building is formed by the load-bearing calcium-silicate brickwork, 175 mm thick, the two central concrete columns and solid flat slabs (no upstand or downstand beams). The timber roof structure rests on steel stanchions. Mineral wool thermal insulation, 180 mm thick, is placed between the rafters. The solid external walls facing north-east have an insulating composite layer, 120 mm thick, on the outside, which is plastered, whereas the south-west elevation of the living rooms is fully glazed. Transparent thermal insulation panels are mounted in front of the solid masonry piers, the outer surfaces of which are painted black.

This transparent insulation allows solar radiation to strike a black absorber wall. The wall heats up and later releases the incident heat energy into the rooms behind. The release of this warmth is controlled through the choice and thickness of the wall material. To achieve a good degree of efficiency, a material with a high bulk density (> 1400 kg/m^3) should be used, such as calcium-silicate brickwork, rubble masonry, stone or concrete. Properly installed systems can be expected to achieve an energy-saving of 100-200 kW/m^2 p.a. (equivalent to 10-20 l heating oil/m^2 p.a.). As transparent thermal insulation can lead to very high wall temperatures, some form of shading to prevent overheating must always be included.

In this project, all transparent glazing comprises heat-absorbing glass with a U value of 1.2 W/m^{2}K. To prevent excessive heating, all windows in the south-west façade have external shades. Ventilation openings are arranged in such a way that cross-ventilation is possible in all directions. The glass panels of transparent thermal insulation in front of the solid masonry piers include an integral shading system. Balconies and canopies are suspended on stainless steel members cast into the floor slabs. Three-ply laminated glass, 34 mm thick, with a non-slip, ceramic ink

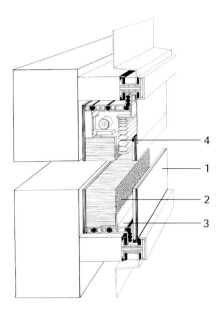

Section, scale 1:5, showing
the make-up of the absorber
wall system: transparent
thermal insulation elements
with integral shading.
Inspection opening at top
with stainless steel cover.

1 Toughened safety glass,
6 mm. 2 Capillary structure,
80 mm. 3 Cavity, 10–
20 mm. 4 Shading provided
by pleated curtain with
closed air chambers and
low-e coating on the inside.

coating, forms the floors to the balconies; being transparent, this allows adequate light through to the living rooms below. The laminated safety glass panes are supported along the edges and held in place by means of individual bolted fixings.

Energy concept

The position of the building enables an optimum solar gain on the south-west side while small openings and good thermal insulation reduce the energy losses on the north-east side. The average U value of the building envelope is less than 0.3 W/m²K and the transmission heat loss remains extremely low. Owing to the storage capacity of the solid elements of the structure, the building develops an extraordinarily moderate temperature behaviour so that a very consistent internal climate ensues. Windows and transparent thermal insulation serve as solar-energy collectors. The black-painted external surfaces of the solid building elements behind the transparent thermal insulation absorb the solar radiation with the shading system open. On a normal, sunny winter's day with the sun at a low altitude, the temperature on the black external surface of the wall rises to about 50°C. Depending on the mass and thickness of the solid wall, the maximum radiated heat on the internal side of the wall is reached after a time lag of 4-6 hours. The temperature of the inner surface of the wall is then about 27-30°C. If there is no further solar radiation, then the temperature gradually drops again within 24 hours. By subtracting the radiation gained from the heating energy requirement due to transmission losses, we get a negative U value for surfaces with transparent thermal insulation for the winter season, i.e. the surfaces gain more energy than is lost through transmission! The heating-up of the wall surfaces not only has an effect on the internal temperature but also on the comfort within the building.

Heating system

A gas condensing boiler, max. output 19 kW, serves as a back-up heating system. This also heats up the 400 l hot-water tank when the flat-plate collectors on the south-west roof can no longer provide sufficient hot water for heating purposes. The heat is distributed via underfloor heating. A ventilation plant with heat recovery was not installed, not only for reasons of cost but also because the transparent thermal insulation system leads to very favourable energy consumption figures; the simulation calculation suggests a figure of approx. 50 kWh/m² p.a.

Graphic of simulation calculation for daylight illumination with light-scattering, transparent thermal insulation elements.

Graphic of simulation calculation for daylight illumination with clear glass.

Simulation calculation

To assess the energy situation and the further development of the building, a thermal simulation calculation was performed. In addition, a daylight simulation calculation was also produced for the living area. Climate data from German test reference year No. 5 (Franconia and northern Baden-Württemberg) was used as the basis for the thermal simulation calculation. This includes hourly figures for air temperature as well as direct and diffuse radiation on a horizontal surface. The building was divided into five thermal zones: living room + kitchen, southern child's room, south-west child's room, attic and other rooms. Use of window ventilation by the occupants was assumed to be as follows: up to 23°C, 0.5-1/h; 23-27°C, 1/h; over 27°C, 2/h, i.e. the volume of air in the room is changed between 0.5 and 2 times every hour. The heating period was defined by a linear 24 h average of the ambient temperature below 15°C. The U values of the building components and the solar-radiation gains of the glazing and the transparent thermal insulation were also included in the calculation. The temperature behaviour was simulated for the summer and for the heating period.

The result of the thermal simulation calculation was that the danger of overheating in summer could be adequately countered by the external shading measures. The average heating requirement was 59 kWh/m² during the heating period. These figures cannot be directly compared with the method of calculation used in the 3rd Thermal Insulation Act; in this case a much lower heating requirement was determined here through back-substitution. The simulation calculation also helped to decide whether transparent thermal insulation daylight systems could be used on the south-east façade and if so, then what amount would be advisable. The graphic output of the computer results shows the lighting intensity distribution for clear glass and light-scattering, transparent thermal insulation daylight elements. Owing to the very high lighting intensity in the living rooms when using transparent thermal insulation elements, as revealed by the computer, a decision was made to restrict the use of transparent thermal insulation to the spandrel panels of the window breast zones.

Transparent thermal insulation

The notion of building a façade out of solar panels was first put forward by Félix Trombe in France, who in 1956 built an experimental house with a glazed heat storage concrete wall in Odeillo-Font in the Pyrenees. The "Kapalux" rebated panels

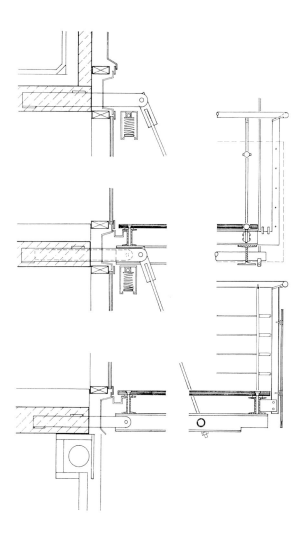

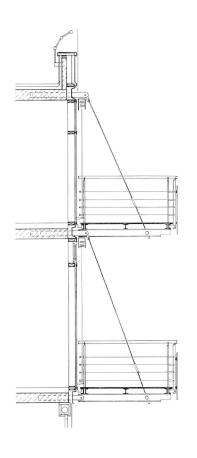

with integral pleated curtains are based on this principle; they are installed in front of the solid wall piers. These transparent thermal insulation elements with integral shading incorporate a capillary structure comprising a multitude of thin-walled tubes, 3.5 mm diameter, made from transparent plastic and arranged perpendicular to the surface. This arrangement serves to scatter the incident radiation. The 80-mm-thick units are enclosed in toughened safety glass panes to both sides, each 6 mm thick.

Six 1300 x 2450 mm and three 1300 x 3000 mm transparent thermal insulation elements were installed. They are placed in front of the black-painted solid wall with a 10-20 mm gap. The integral shading ensures that the façade is as cool as a conventional façade in summer. The transparent thermal insulation elements used in this project have pressure compensation ports. However, in another residential project designed by the architects, the transparent thermal insulation units have hermetically sealed edges and a noble-gas filling. The advantage of these units compared to those with pressure compensation ports is that they are about 50% thinner for the same k value and are easier to handle. The thickness is just 49 mm. The dimensions of the "Kapalux" H-panels is min. 1000 x 1000 mm to max. 1200 x 2500 mm. In this case, an external sunshade is fitted for the necessary summer shading. Properly installed systems can be expected to achieve an energy gain through transparent thermal insulation of 100-200 kWh/m^2 p.a. (equivalent to 10-20 l heating oil/m^2 p.a.).

Balcony, scale 1:75.

The steelwork of the balcony is suspended on stainless steel members cast into the floor slabs. The balcony floors are 3-ply laminated safety glass, 34 mm thick, with a non-slip, ceramic ink coating. The glass is fastened by means of individual bolted fixings.

Detail of balcony, scale 1:30.

Section,
scale 1:1000.

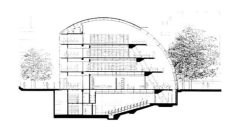

Plan, 2nd floor,
scale 1:1000.

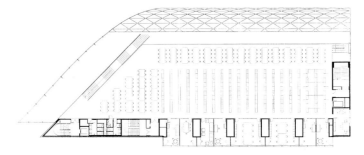

Plan, 1st floor,
scale 1:1000.

Plan, ground floor,
scale 1:1000.

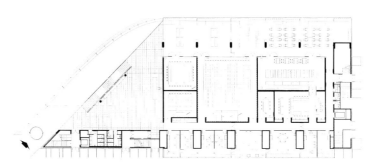

West elevation; behind, the
four-storey staircase.

Stairs with glazed balustrading in the atrium at the
transition from curved
northern to vertical western
façade.

Curved north elevation with triangular insulating glass units, side lengths 3.8 x 2.8 m, mounted using the structural silicone system. In the background, the Faculty of History by James Stirling.

61

Faculty of Law, Cambridge University
Sir Norman Foster

In May 1990 the architects succeeded in winning the competition to design a new home for the faculty and the Institute for Criminology. The design provided for two pavilions; however, with the consent of the university, the plans were altered in favour of one joint building, which was completed in 1995. The 9,000 m² of this one building contain five lecture theatres, meeting rooms, students' recreation rooms, offices and the Squire Library with its stock of 120,000 books. About 1,000 students and 100 staff can be accommodated on the six floors, two of which are below ground level.

The shape of the building reflects its urban setting. Therefore, the west elevation, set back from the longitudinal axis at an angle of 45°, is parallel with the Faculty of History by James Stirling opposite and opens out towards the northern park area to the west. The plain south elevation corresponds with the stone faculty building by Casson Conder opposite. A curved glass wall faces onto the northern park area. The main entrance in the south-west corner leads to a glazed atrium which extends from basement to roof linking all floors to each other. Adjacent to the atrium at basement level are students' recreation rooms and three lecture theatres, at ground floor level the foyer leading to teaching area and offices, and at first floor level the reception of the library. The atrium ensures that plenty of daylight reaches all these areas. The library occupies the top three floors. The reading rooms run alongside the curved glass wall, allowing a view of the gardens outside and providing even lighting from a northerly direction.

Design and glazing

Rising up at an angle from the basement foundations are five concrete columns which carry the cantilevers on the northern side of the three concrete floor slabs. The supporting structure for the curved northern façade is a Vierendeel girder – spanning almost 40 m – made of steel sections in a triangular arrangement on which the glazing is mounted. The 240 identical, stepped insulating glass units are also triangular, with side lengths of 3800 x 2800 mm. These units, made up of 10 mm toughened safety glass, a 14 mm cavity and 12.76 mm laminated safety glass, are factory-glued into aluminium frames using a structural silicone system.

Location
Faculty of Law, Cambridge University, West Road, UK

Client
Cambridge University

Architects
Sir Norman Foster & Partners, London

Project team
Sir Norman Foster, Spencer de Grey, John Silver, Chris Connel, Michael Jones, Mouzhan Majdi, Giuseppe Boscherini, Angus Campbell, Glenis Fan, Jason Flanagan, Lucy Highton, Ben Marshall, Divya Patel, Kate Peak, Victoria Pike, Austin Relton, Giles Robinson, John Small, Ken Wai, Cindy Walters, Ricarda Zimmerer

Structural engineers
YMR Anthony Hunt Associates

Glazing
Brüder Eckelt & Co., Steyr, Austria

Façade
Metallbau Früh GmbH, Umkirch

Date of completion
1995

Some of the glazing units are provided with a non-coloured, solar-control coating. The pre-assembled glazing elements were attached to aluminimum supports fixed to the external steelwork. Six-part nodes form the joints between steelwork and glazing units. These joints can move in three directions in order to take up tolerances. The curved glass of the façade changes to a stainless steel roof covering at the ridge. Parts of the east and west elevations are also glazed, with "Litex-Design" shading and antiglare features being included from the start of the planning. The southern façade is clad partly in stone, while the offices on this side are provided with translucent, printed glass and transparent zones with opening windows. An interesting glass interior detail is the horizontal, loadbearing and fire-resistant glazing at ground floor level in front of the curved glass façade, which directs daylight into the basement.

A curved transition panel links curved and vertical façades and accommodates the thermal movements of both.

Ground floor foyer. The glazed lightwell in front of the glass façade is capable of taking pedestrian traffic. Glazing: laminated safety glass, 52 mm thick.

Detail, scale 1:7,5. Junction between curved and vertical glass façade.

1 Silicone seal profile.
2 Aluminium angle, 3 mm.
3 Thermal insulation. 4 M5 x 45. 5 M6 x 45. 6 M10 x 60.
7 Waterproofing, 0.5 mm.
8 "Compriband". 9 Aluminium disc, 30 mm ø.
10 Insulating glass.

Section A–B.

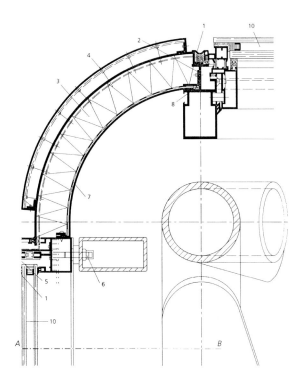

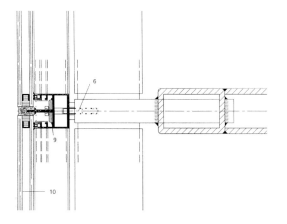

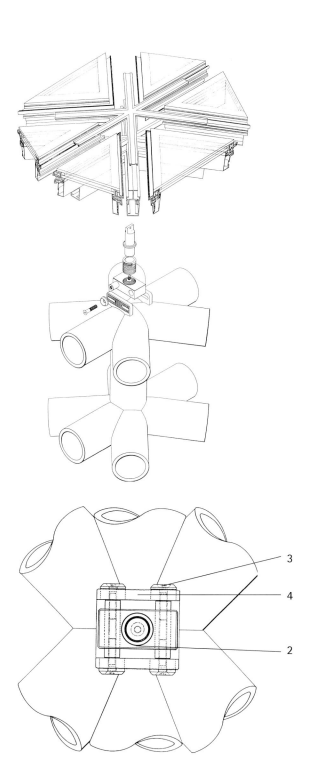

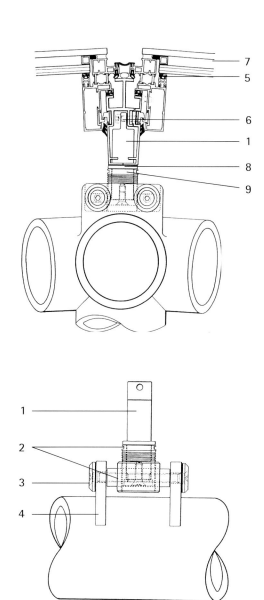

Isometric view of junction between steelwork and glass façade.

Details of 6-part node.

1 Steel bolt, ø 34 mm.
2 Threaded pin. 3 Serrated aluminium washer, ø 41 mm.
4 Support lugs. 5 Silicone sealant. 6 Hexagon-socket screw, M8 x 30. 7 Insulating glass. 8 Aluminium disc, ø 40 x 6 mm. 9 M5 x 16.

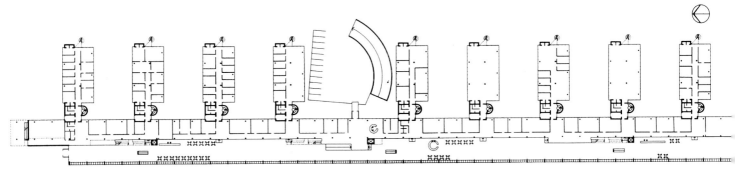

Plan of ground floor,
scale 1:1500.

Site plan, scale 1:3000. The
circular building at the
southern end was not
constructed.

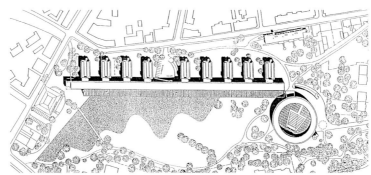

Isometric view.

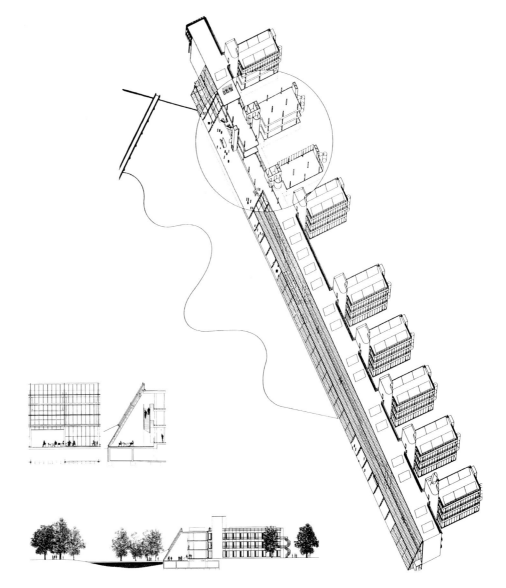

Arcade, part elevation and
section, scale 1:750.

Section, scale 1:1500.

The 274-m-long glass arcade serves as access concourse, communication zone and exhibition area. Vierendeel girders spaced at 7.2 m support the bays of the column-and-beam façade, which is glazed with "Thermoplus neutral" heat-absorbing glass.

Technology Centre in Science Park, Gelsenkirchen
Uwe Kiessler + Partner

The science park facility is a project of the Emscher Park International Building Exhibition within the framework of the restructuring of the Ruhr district in the west of Germany. Today, this region, where the mining industry once prevailed over generations, can no longer rely on coalmining and steel production to give it a foundation. Instead, new technologies and research as to the industries of the future are creating a modern economic platform for this area. The 30-hectare site of the new science park was once dominated by the Zeche Rheinelbe mine, whose first shaft was sank here in 1855, and the Thyssen steelworks, until the buildings were pulled down in 1985. The only reminder left standing is the administration block dating from 1918, which has been restored and now houses the local industrial relations tribunal.

The long form of the Technology Centre is situated on the eastern side of the site next to an artificial lake. A 300-m-long institute building forms the main axis, linking together the nine chamber-like, three-storey pavilions facing the Munscheidstrasse. Each floor of these buildings offers 270 m² of usable space, which is rented out to businesses, research centres and design institutes. The aim here is to achieve a concentration of those companies, institutes and laboratories dealing with research into renewable energy sources as well as their development and application. In total, the Technology Centre has 10,000 m² of floor space available to let. The building was awarded the 1995 German Architecture Prize.

Glass arcade

The 274-m-long glass arcade running north-south overlooks the landscaped park and artificial lake to the west. This side is fully glazed and inclined at an angle of 58°. The arcade is open to the public and serves as main access concourse, communication zone and exhibition area. Stairs lead up from the floor to galleries giving access to offices and conference rooms as well as the nine pavilions on the eastern side.

The column-and-beam façade of the arcade is supported by steelwork in the form of Vierendeel girders at a spacing of 7.20 m and inclined to follow the slope of the glazing. The Fraunhofer Institute for Solar Energy Systems in Freiburg was con-

Location
Wissenschaftspark und Technologiezentrum Rheinelbe, Munscheidstrasse 14, 45886 Gelsenkirchen, Germany

Clients
State of North Rhine-Westfalia, Wissenschaftspark Rheinelbe, Gelsenkirchner Vermögensgesellschaft mbH

Architects
Kiessler & Partner, Munich
Uwe Kiessler, Hermann Schultz

Assistance
Konstanze Elbel, Andreas Gierer, Stefanie Reithwiesner

Structural engineers
Sailer, Stepan, Bloos, Munich

Building services
Ing.-Büro Trumpp, Gräfelfing

Electrical installation
Ingenieurgemeinschaft Riemhofer und Zerull, Munich

Energy Concept
Fraunhofer Institute for Solar Energy Systems, Freiburg

Photovoltaic system
Pilkington Solar International, Cologne

Glass construction
Helmut Fischer GmbH, Talheim

Date of completion
1995

The long, slim form of the west side with its glass arcade lies on the banks of an artificial lake.

Part of the west façade.

sulted with regard to the internal climate of the arcade. The institute recommended that large fresh-air inlets be provided at the base and small exhaust-air outlets at the top. Following this advice, the bottommost bays of the façade, approx. 7 m wide and 4.5 m high, were constructed as sliding elements with electric motors to raise them upwards. Therefore, the entire length of the arcade can be opened on the park side in summer. Together with the opening vents at roof level, this achieves permanent, draught-free ventilation, which can be further assisted by the smoke vents installed to satisfy the fire regulations.

The arcade is glazed with "Thermoplus Neutral" thermal insulation glass which, owing to the construction, is in the form of stepped insulating glass with a UV-resistant edge seal. The outer, larger pane consists of 6 mm toughened safety glass. The shading screen glued to the drip course partly conceals the beams of the supporting structure. The inner pane of laminated safety glass, 8 mm thick with reinforced interlayer, holds splinters of glass in place. The cavity between the panes measures 12 mm; filling with a noble gas is not possible because the UV-resistant silicone sealant used for the edge seal is not sufficiently gastight and the gas would gradually escape. An infrared-reflecting, low-emissivity coating is applied to the inside of the inner pane. The U value of this glazing is 2.0 W/m^2K and the g-value 62%.

The dynamic simulation calculations carried out by the Fraunhofer Institute to establish the heating requirement and temperature behaviour of the building reveal quite clearly that the greatest heat savings can be achieved by reducing the air-changes affecting energy use both in the arcade and in the adjoining rooms and offices. Likewise, major savings are possible by reducing the temperature at night in the arcade and in the rooms and offices, and by reducing the temperature at weekends in the rooms and offices. The simulations also showed that by reducing the temperature in the arcade to 18°C, compared with the standard figure of 20°C, heating energy savings of about 25% are possible. Heating energy consumption for the arcade is 85 kWh/m^2 p.a. The underfloor heating to the arcade also permits cooling in summer.

The external shading in front of the inclined glass wall is controlled centrally like all other sunshading systems around the building. Split up according to compass direction, the shading systems are monitored via sensors as well as wind and rain detectors. In addition, it is possible to regulate the shades by means of the external temperature. The controls for the drive motors for the arcade as well as the actuators for the opening windows are housed in a duct at the top of the glazing, accessible from the roof.

Solar power plant

A photovoltaic plant for generating electricity from solar radiation is installed on the roof of the Technology Centre. This comprises 900 solar panels each 810 x 2090 mm mounted on 75 galvanized steel frames, inclined 28° to the south. The concrete foundations to the frames are simply placed on the roof and not fixed down. This method could be used to install solar panels on existing roofs, provided they can carry the loads.

The total area of the panels is 1521 m², the area of the solar cells 1236 m². With a peak output of 210 kW_p, the plant delivers about 190,000 kWh per year. This corresponds to the electricity requirements of 40 four-person households! The system marks the first industrial use of the monocrystalline silicon solar cell by BP Solar, 123 x 123 mm in size. This new type of cell converts up to 17% of the incident solar radiation into electricity. Up to now, conventional cells achieved degrees of efficiency of between 13 and 15%.

The solar cells for the solar panels on the Technology Centre are manufactured using a new technique which embeds the cells in a special casting resin between two panes of glass. The outer pane of this composite element consists of toughened, low iron oxide, colourless glass, the inner pane of toughened float glass. The

The bottommost bays of the façade, approx. 7 m wide and 4.5 m high, are constructed as sliding elements with electric motors to raise them upwards.

View through opened façade beneath extended awning.

West façade with sunshading in position; it can be extended out like an awning in front of the bottommost bays.

The glass wall to the arcade is inclined at 58°. Maintenance is by means of a trolley, the bottom ladder section of which can be retracted.

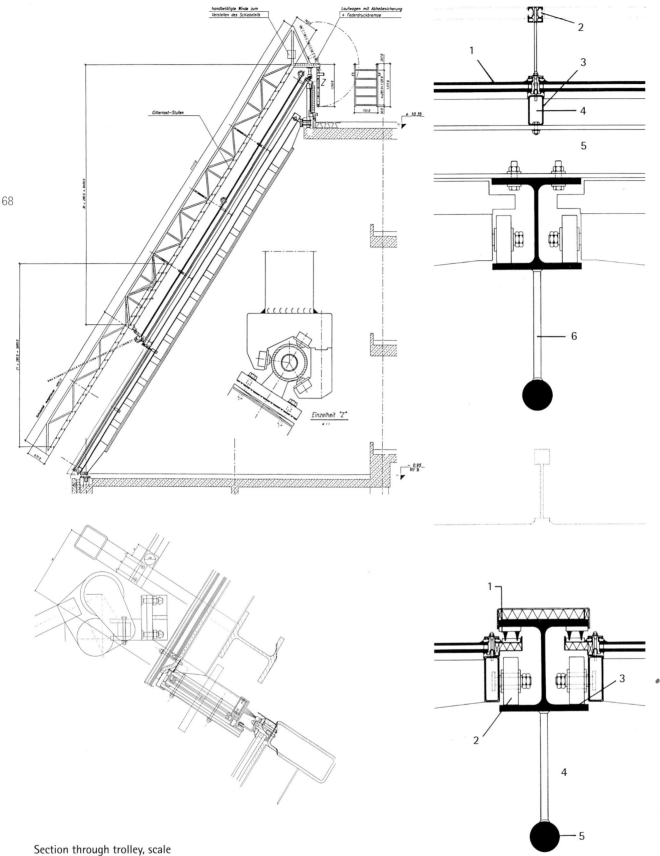

Section through trolley, scale 1:100. The detail at scale 1:3 shows the mobile unit with spring-pressure brake and device to safeguard against uplift.

Horizontal section through main girder, arcade façade, scale 1:10.

Top, fixed glazing: 1 Heat-absorbing glass. 2 Guide for fabric sunshade. 3 Column-and-beam construction. 4 Hollow section, 80 x 40 mm. 5 Purlin, HEB 140. 6 Steel flat.

Bottom, sliding element: 1 Spandrel panel. 2 Roller for sliding element. 3 Steel section, HEB 240. 4 Vierendeel girder. 5 Round steel bar, ø 80 mm.

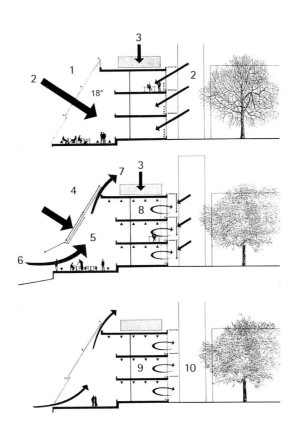

Schematic diagram of climate concept.

Top, winter's day:
1 Heat-absorbing glass, U = 1.3 W/m²K. 2 Solar heat gain. 3 Solar power plant.

Centre, summer's day:
4 External sunshading. 5 Hinged element opened. 6 Fresh air. 7 Exhaust air. 8 Heat absorbed by storage media.

Bottom, summer's night:
9 Night-time cooling of heat storage media. 10 Rainproof vents.

layer of casting resin is transparent. With an area of 1.7 m², the panels used at the Technology Centre are larger by far than those available hitherto, which had a maximum area of 1.2 m². In fact, the new manufacturing process of Pilkington Solar International can produce panels of up to 6 m²! Photovoltaic elements of this kind can be installed in insulating glass units in façades and inclined glazing; in combination with appropriate panes on the inside they can fulfil additional functions such as safety, light-scattering, acoustic and thermal insulation.

The photovoltaic plant at the Technology Centre is the first system of this size to employ a modular d.c./a.c. converter concept, thus increasing the overall flexibility and degree of efficiency. This device converts the d.c. electricity produced by the solar cells into a.c. electricity. With a low level of solar radiation, four small 5 kW converters are used. As the level of solar radiation increases, the large 160 kW 12-pulse thyristor convertor cuts in; this operates best at higher outputs.

The lifetime of this photovoltaic plant is estimated to be about 30 years. The total cost of the system – DM 6 million – was financed by the European Union (DM 2.4 million from the "THERMIE" programme), the state of North Rhine-Westphalia (DM 2.4 million from the programme for rational energy usage and the use of inexhaustible energy sources) and RWE Energie AG (DM 1.2 million from the photovoltaic programme).

A total of 900 solar panels, 810 x 2090 mm, on 75 galvanized steel frames are installed on the roof. They supply 190,000 kWh of electricity. The concrete foundations to the frames are simply placed on the roof without being fixed down. This method could be used to install solar panels on existing roofs, provided they can carry the loads.

View of the entrance to the museum.

Laminated safety glass columns along the external wall form the supports for the laminated safety glass beams. The striped pattern of baked-on ceramic ink serves to protect against the sun. It increases in density from the outside toward the inside.

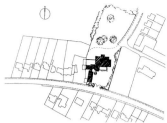

Inside the museum entrance. The striped pattern on the roof glazing, combined with solar-control glass, reduces solar radiation transmittance to 37%.

Museum of Glass, Kingswinford
Design Antenna

Broadfield House is a 19th-century listed building. It had served as a private clinic until it became the home for a collection of English glass dating from the 18th and 19th centuries. In the autumn of 1993 a national competition led to the architects being awarded the contract to renew the internal facilities and add a visitors' entrance at the rear of the building. The architects decided to use the new entrance extension to demonstrate the role of glass in architecture; the contemporary use of the material contrasting with the historic collection. Brent Richards explains: "Architecturally, it was our intention to find a subtle solution which would express glass technology but would not be so striking that it dominated the existing building." And as to the listed building status, Richards comments: "One of our arguments for not wanting to erect a reflective box or coloured structure on the rear side of the building was that we felt it did not correspond with the contemporary use of glass but instead was very much associated with the 1970s. We proposed a transparent solution which would allow the visitor to see the listed building through the new construction. Luckily, the person responsible from the listed buildings office supported our philosophy and approved the concept." The Duke of Gloucester opened the renovated museum in November 1994. Since then, the glass pavilion has been nominated for six awards.

Materials and design
The extension is 11 m long, 3.5 m high and 5.7 m wide. It is attached to the brick rear wall of the existing building. The side walls are formed by the existing brickwork on one side and a new solid wall on the other. The glass construction itself is relatively simple: glass beams, 5.7 m long and 300 mm deep, span from the rear wall onto glass columns, 3.5 m high and 200 mm deep, spaced at 1.1 m centres along the glass front wall. The glass beams and columns are made from laminated safety glass comprising three 10 mm glass panes. As the beams were too long for the autoclaves available to enable production with PVB interlayers, they were laminated with catalyst-cured resin and so have a total thickness of 32 mm. The glass beams are mounted in steel hanger brackets on the rear wall. The connection between beam and column is by means of a mortise-and-tenon joint, bonded on site

Location
Broadfield House,
Kingswinford, UK

Client
Dudley Metropolitan Borough Council

Architects
Design Antenna, London
Brent G. Richards, Robert Dabell

Structural engineers
Dewhurst Macfarlane
& Partners, London

Laminated glass
F.A. Firman, Romford

Glazing
Solarglas, Bradford

Date of completion
1994

Glass wall made from insulating glass with toughened solar-control glass ("Cool-Lite" K 169). Roof overhang with stepped insulating glass in which the upper pane of 10 mm solar-control glass projects.

Plan of ground floor.

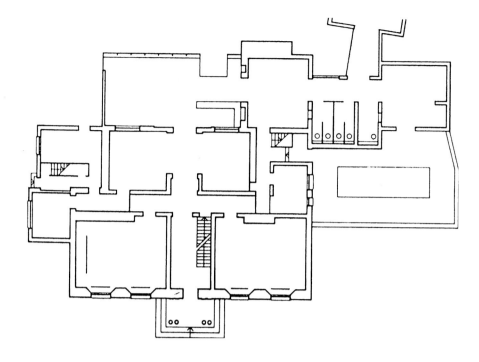

with casting resin. As the extension is situated on the south-west side, the roof was made from insulating glass units, 3.7 x 1 m, comprising a non-coloured, solar-control glass, 10 mm thick (St Gobain, "Cool-Lite" K 169), a 10 mm cavity and an inner pane of laminated safety glass, 11.9 mm thick, the inside pane of which is toughened and printed with a striped pattern. This combination of glasses reduces solar radiation transmittance to 37%. The U value of the total insulating glazing is 1.7 W/m²K. The insulating glass units forming the roof glazing employ silicone to glue them to the beams and seal the roof watertight.

The glass roof has a pitch of 1.5° to the rear wall and is designed for a snow load of 0.75 kN/m² so that it is also accessible for cleaning. The front elevation consists of insulating glass units, 3.7 x 1.1 m, comprising toughened solar-control glass, 8 mm thick ("Cool-Lite" K 169 neutral), a 10 mm cavity and toughened safety glass, 10 mm thick. This combination of glasses has transmittance values of 59% for solar radiation and 61% for daylight. The two leaves of the all-glass door are positioned beneath a 2.2-m-long box-section glass lintel.

Glass as a structural material

All in all, this intriguing all-glass construction has something of an experimental character too. Glass is employed here as a structural material, mainly subjected to compression. The compressive strength of glass is very high, reaching 700-900 N/mm² (according to DIN 51067, Part 1). Just as a comparison, Granite has a compressive strength of max. 250 N/mm² and cast iron 700-850 N/mm². However, the tensile bending strength – just 45 N/mm² – is low in comparison. The current permissible tensile strength in Germany is 30-35 N/mm², fixed by the respective building inspectorate. The reason for this is to be found in DIN 1249, Part 10: "The tensile bending strength of glass is not a material constant; its measured value, like with all brittle materials, is far more influenced by the nature of the surface subjected to tension. Microscopic and macroscopic surface damage diminish the measured value for tensile bending strength. The result is that the term 'tensile bending strength' can only be defined statistically by means of a reliable value for probability of fracture. For a given tension, the probability of fracture depends on the size of the surface subjected to tension and the duration of the loading. The definition of tensile bending strength means there is a 95% chance that those tensile bending stresses which lead to a probability of fracture of 5% are greater than the values given in Table 2 (45 N/mm^2)."

The main method of increasing the poor tensile bending strength of glass is to temper it by heating it up to 600°C and then cooling it rapidly. This causes the outside surfaces to solidify faster, while the core is still hot and soft, which means that the outside surfaces are under compression and the core under tension. This raises the tensile bending strength to 120 N/mm^2 while the compressive strength remains at 700-900 N/mm^2. Design calculations in Germany are based on 50 N/mm^2. To achieve some residual strength upon breakage, laminated safety glass is used, like in this glass pavilion; this contains a viscoplastic PVB interlayer which holds the broken pieces of glass together. The glass beams of the pavilion were a problem because the glass panes are laminated with catalyst-cured resin and not by PVB. Autoclaves, in which the bond between the glass and the PVB interlayer is created under heat and pressure, come in many different sizes. Therefore, the maximum dimensions for laminated safety glass vary enormously from manufacturer to manufacturer. On average, the maximum length of glass that can be handled is 5 m. However, there is one autoclave in Germany which can handle pieces up to 1.7 x 7.2 m (at BGT in Bretten).

Had this pavilion been on German soil, then it is doubtful whether "approval for an individual project", i.e. a licence to build in an exceptional case, would have been granted for the all-glass construction. On the other hand, such an experimental solution is an example of what really can be accomplished with glass. However, such a design requires a great deal of skill and knowledge in design and construction; hasty imitations are not recommended! A great deal of research is still required in the field of using glass as a structural material in order to be able to count on more dependable material values. However, the evolution of glass technology and glass construction during the 20th century has demonstrated that it is precisely challenges like this glass pavilion that can lead to the exploration of new paths.

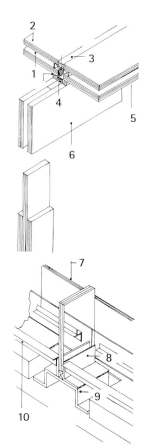

73

Isometric view of upper connection between insulating glass roofing panels, beams and columns – both laminated safety glass – (top) and isometric view of base of glass column (bottom).

1 Cavity, 10 mm, silicone seal. 2 Toughened solar-control glass. 3 Silicone seal. 4 Spacer. 5 Laminated safety glass, 2 x 6 mm. 6 Glass beam, 32 mm thick. 7 Solar-control insulating glass. 8 Steel angle. 9 Steel bracket. 10 T-section.

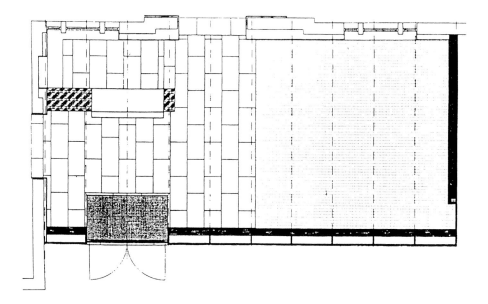

Plan of entrance pavilion.

The basement is lit from one side via the low-level yard. Glass façade with opened sunshading.

Section through atrium and low-level yard, scale 1:500. In the centre, the area of planting; on the right, the pond. The "sunsail" is above the sliding roof.

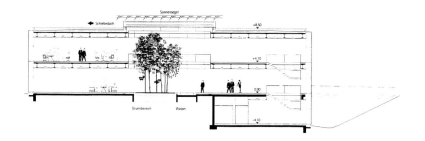

Plan of ground floor, scale 1:500.

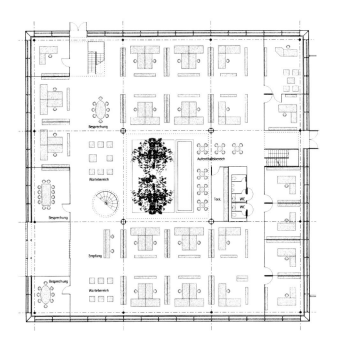

Head office of GÖTZ GmbH, Würzburg
Webler + Geissler

The aim behind the design and layout of the office building for this medium-sized metal fabrication company was to combine optimum use of energy with a high degree of comfort and good working conditions. This was achieved with a compact, fully glazed envelope to the building and an open atrium. The two-storey frame structure with in-situ basement measures 40 x 40 m in plan and is 8.4 m high. Roof and intermediate floors are of steelwork with composite floor slabs. The large internal volume with low proportion of external surface area minimizes heat losses through transmission. Clear storey heights of 3.2 m and the above-average, generously sized workplaces result in volumes of air which are so large that air-change rates, and hence heat losses through ventilation, can be kept low during unfavourable weather conditions.

   The ground floor contains the offices of the management and the commercial staff. Besides a spacious open-plan layout, separate, quieter rooms are available for meetings. The upper floor is again open-plan and accommodates the development department and engineering staff. The basement, lit from one side via a low-level yard, houses training, staff and storage rooms as well as the plant room containing important components of the total energy system. The fully glazed roof over the central atrium can be raised and moved. This enables draught-free ventilation and night-time cooling in the middle of summer. With extensive planting and a pond, the 12 x 12 m atrium not only contributes to a better climate in the form of an oxygen reservoir and air humidifier but also to the general well-being of the occupants.

Double-skin glass façade

Up to 40% of the total energy consumed in office blocks these days is just for artificial lighting! Better use of daylight can save a substantial amount of this energy. The large areas of glass in this building as well as the glass-roofed atrium serve to make better use of daylight and, in addition, capture the total incident solar radiation. The double-skin façade acts as a climate buffer between the interior and exterior. With the help of reflector and absorber louvres, vents, recirculation fans and control technology in this 600 mm cavity, the façade can react promptly and effi-

Location
GÖTZ GmbH, Delpstrasse 4-6,
97084 Würzburg, Germany

Client
GÖTZ GmbH, Würzburg

Architects
Martin Webler and Garnet Geissler, Stuttgart

Building management system
GÖTZ GmbH, Marcus Püttmer

Structural engineers
Ing.-Büro R. Wolff, Stuttgart

Date of completion
1995

The glazed separating wall
of laminated safety glass,
2 x 8 mm, in elevation
(scale 1:60) and in horizontal section (scale 1:30).

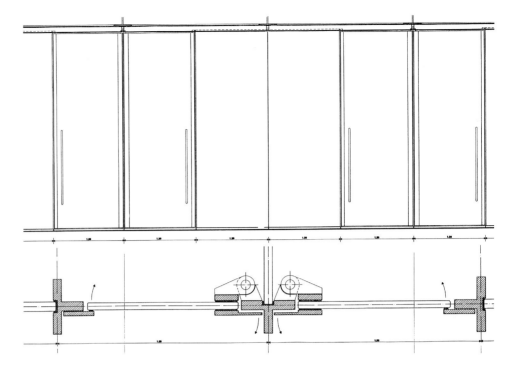

Isometric view of façade
structure. Outer glazing
with insulating glass (8/14/
6 mm). Inner glazing with
solar-control insulating glass
(8 mm float glass, 14 mm
cavity, 6 mm toughened
safety glass with low-
emissivity coating. The
U value of the façade is
approx. 0.8 W/m^{2}K.

Schematic diagram of
climatic principles.

Section through façade,
scale 1:25. The façade
cavity is 600 mm wide.

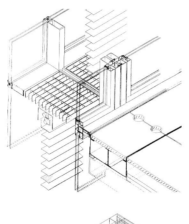

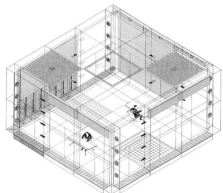

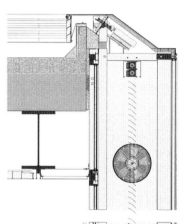

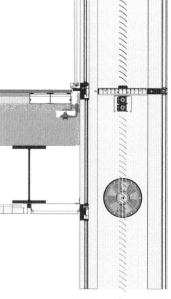

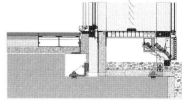

ciently to changing climatic conditions. The outer skin comprises fixed glazing, with the intake of fresh air into the cavity regulated by adjustable vents at ground and roof levels. The inner skin of glass contains sliding doors which allow individuals to determine their own local climate. The outer glazing is insulating glass (8/14/8 mm). The inner glazing consists of insulating glass units made up of 8 mm float glass, 14 mm cavity and 6 mm toughened safety glass with a low-emissivity coating. The U value of the whole façade is 0.8 W/m²K.

To achieve a high level of daylighting with optimum sunshading, two louvre elements, one suspended above the other, regulate the incoming light. The upper louvres are used to reflect sunlight and the angular positions of the reflector as well as the lower, absorber louvres can be independently controlled. The absorber louvres provide excellent protection against glare when the sun is low. As each louvre is perforated, vision is not impeded, even when the louvres are closed. At night the lower louvres are rotated 180° to reflect the internal lighting back into the building. When the outside temperature is low, the vents are closed so that a "cushion" of warm air surrounds the building. Only on the side facing the sun does fresh air enter the cavity and warm up on the absorber louvres. This warm air is then fed into the interior by fans located in the corners of the building. In summer the louvres are closed and their reflective surfaces turned outwards, thus reflecting most of the incident light back through the glass before it can be converted into long-wave infrared radiation. Convection currents create a stack effect; the fresh air entering at ground level rises and is exhausted through the open upper vent as waste heat.

Cooling

With vents and sliding doors open, the lower temperatures in the night can be used for cooling. In addition, the building is cooled by means of solar energy. An adsorp-

Ground floor meeting room behind fully glazed walls of laminated safety glass, 2 x 8 mm thick.

Ground floor open-plan office. On the left, the glass stairs with treads of laminated safety glass, 3 x 10 mm, with non-slip printing. Stair balustrading is 10 mm toughened safety glass.

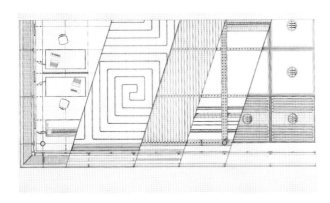

Schematic diagram of floor showing the various layers. From left to right: plan of office, underfloor heating, composite floor slab, steel-work, cooling/reflective ceiling.

Model with opened glass roof under planned shading louvres.

Fabric ceiling panel for improving the internal acoustics.

The cooling ceiling panel can also be used for heating.

Fans at the corners of the façade cavity distribute warm air from the sunlit side right around the building.

tion heat pump is driven by hot water from thermal solar collectors whose maximum output is available exactly when cooling is needed. The cooling is achieved via the pipes of the underfloor heating system working in reverse and via newly developed grid ceiling panels. The large surface area of the cooling grid panels, open at the top, prevents condensation problems despite high specific output, and at the same time enables the thermal activation of the energy-storing solid floor slab above. The cooling ceiling panels are only placed near the double-skin façade and in the atrium. To improve the internal acoustics, 2.4 x 2.4 m fabric ceiling panels are used for sound attenuation.

Heating

The building is heated by a small combined power plant which converts primary energy into both electrical and heating energy. The latter is fed via a water circuit directly into the underfloor heating or temporarily stored in seasonal storage media ready for use as required. Owing to their fast reaction time, the cooling ceilings can also be used as a back-up heat source for the underfloor heating, which reacts much more sluggishly. On a clear winter's day, the heating need only be switched on when the outside temperature drops to 0°C! Internal loads and solar heat gain are sufficient to maintain the building at operating temperature. The electrical energy generated by the power plant is fed mainly to the company's production plant adjacent the offices.

Control

The building management system makes use of a bus, i.e. a wiring system for transmitting data and control signals, linked to a master computer. The software for this is essentially based on a fuzzy-logic module. This fuzzy logic enables control with undefined limits, i.e. a multitude of influencing variables can be handled simultane-

ously. Left to operate over a period of time, the neuronal network gathers more and more data and so gradually optimizes the control to match the real behaviour of the building. Some 250 sensors and over 1000 actuators provide the building management system with information and enable the control to react accordingly. Besides general weather data such as wind direction, windspeed, rain, outside temperature and outside air humidity, information from inside the building is also collated, e.g. presence of people, lighting intensity, air temperature and humidity. This wealth of data is then used by the master computer to switch on and off the solar collectors, combined power plant, refrigerating machine, underfloor heating, cooling ceilings and artificial lighting. The louvre panels, vents, sliding doors and fans in the façade cavity are all kept at the optimum setting.

Glass in interior works

It is not only the façades which are extremely transparent. Inside the building too, transparency is a key design factor, with separating walls, doors, stair treads, balustrading and spandrel panels all being made completely from glass in order to make maximum use of daylight. The two glass stairs have treads of laminated safety glass, 3 x 10 mm, with non-slip printing. Separating walls are made from zone-toughened, laminated safety glass, 2 x 8 mm. Spandrel panels and balustrading to the stairs are toughened safety glass.

This innovative building has already won a number of awards, including the 1996 Balthasar-Neumann Prize and the 1996 Prize of the Bavarian Section of the Federation of German Architects (BDA).

Sectional elevation, scale 1:750, showing the secondary construction and the installations on the internal blocks.

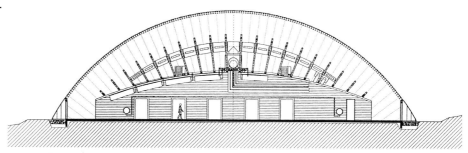

Plan of hall, scale 1:750.

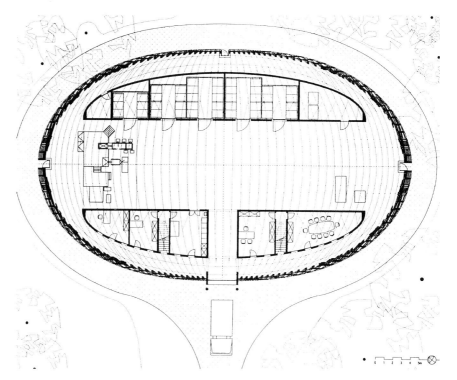

Section with details of frame structure, scale 1:100 and 1:20.

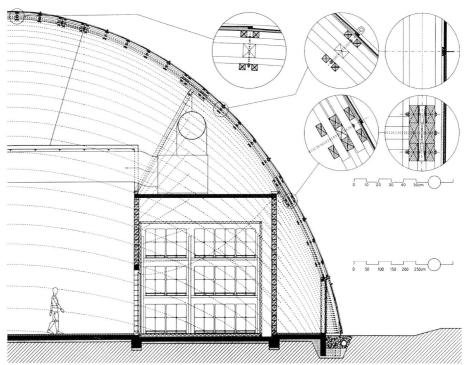

Wallonia Forestry Centre, Marche-en-Famenne
Philippe Samyn

This forestry centre for the preparation of tree seeds lies among 200-year-old oaks in the heart of the thickly wooded Ardennes. The site is near the Aye industrial estate which borders the N4 motorway at Marche-en-Famenne. The regional administration of Wallonia wanted a structure which expressed its dynamic plans for the future and its consideration for the environment; it should be an economic building exploiting the progress made in timber construction. The centre comprises a workroom for the drying, storage and treatment of seeds, as well as a group of cold storage rooms, offices and laboratories. These are all combined in one glazed, egg-shaped hall, 43 m long, 27 m wide and 12.47 m high. The shape is the result of the interaction of function, internal climate requirements, structural concept and the desire for an economical building with low costs and simple maintenance.

Materials and design

The three-dimensional frame to the hall consists of curved timber elements. Wood as a construction material has a long tradition; for example, the yurt tents of the Mongolians or the roundhouses of the Zulus. Interest in this type of construction was rekindled in 1975 with the lattice timber shell of the multipurpose hall in Mannheim, Germany, by Carlfried Mutschler and Joachim Langner with Frei Otto, the timber construction college in Dorset, England, in 1982 by Ahrends, Burton & Koralek with Edmund Happold, and Kiyonori Kikutake's Pavilions for the 1988 "Silk Routes" exhibition in Nara, Japan. Philippe Samyn's original idea was to bend indigenous, still-green timber. However, detailed studies and trials proved that the wood split upon subsequent drying. Therefore, kiln-dried timber was bent using steam, impregnated with insecticides and subsequently re-dried.

The principle element of the hall structure is a double-layer arch of square-section members, 6.14 and 6.21 m long, with various cross-sections. The arches run both lengthwise and transversely in order to achieve stiffness in all directions. Horizontal forces are also absorbed by the secondary constructions on the two internal blocks housing offices, laboratories and cold storage rooms flanking the central "nave" along the longitudinal axis. The timber construction has a net volume of 114 m³ of wood and encloses an area of 960 m² and a volume of 6500 m³.

Location
Comptoir Wallon de Matériels
Forestiers de Reproduction,
Marche-en-Famenne, Belgium

Client
Executive Regional Wallon,
Jambes

Design and structural engineering
Samyn et Associés sprl,
Bruxelles

Philippe Samyn, R. Delaunoit,
D. Melotte, G. André

Curved timber members
Koos & Cie sa, Lierneux

Timber construction
Mesuiserie Fréson sc, Lonein

Glazing
Portal sa, Brussels

Date of completion
1995

Model of glass fixing.

Design sketch of glass fixing.

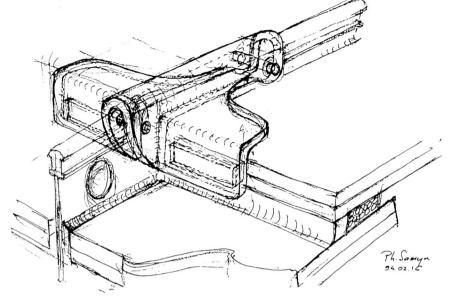

Horizontal forces are taken by the secondary construction on the internal block.

Interior view with side corridor.

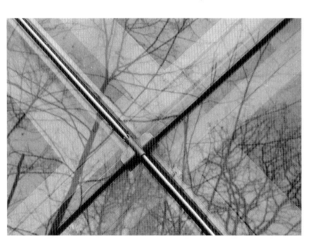

A special glass fixing made from aluminium serves to hold the laminated safety glass with its solar-control coating.

Roof glazing

The timber structure is covered with a skin of laminated safety glass. Philippe Samyn, together with Portal, the Belgian glass construction firm, developed a fixing especially for this project. Aluminimum T-sections are mounted on the transverse timber arches. The trapezoidal panes of glass are placed on these with silicone sealant on two sides and overlapping like scales in the longitudinal direction. Aluminium clips, screwed onto the T-sections, serve as fixings. The overlaps are also sealed with silicone. The 2035 trapezoidal panes of laminated safety glass (totalling 1572 m²) come in 250 different sizes, ranging from 972 x 528 mm to 982 x 1021 mm. They were manufactured according to drawings and templates. The make-up of the glass is as follows: an outer pane of metal oxide coated, solar-control glass with a silvery, neutral reflection, a PVB interlayer and an inner pane of float glass. The pyrolysis coating (hard coating) is on the inside. The average shading coefficient (b-factor) is 0.56 and hence roughly corresponds to the shading provided by a textile membrane. This b-factor expresses the proportion of solar energy which passes through a glass and into the room beyond. The basis for this figure is the solar heat gain via 3 mm clear glass with a constant g-value (total energy transmittance) of 87%. The b-factor is the basis for calculating the cooling load. The smaller the factor, the better the sunshading effect. In this building, the shading (b-factor of 0.56) is sufficient to prevent the timber from overheating. Incidentally, the timber structure itself offers plenty of shading in summer and the surrounding deciduous forest also contributes towards protecting against excessive amounts of solar radiation.

The building is ventilated and heated to provide a pleasant internal climate. Fans can be used to reinforce the ventilation in order to disperse any ensuing humidity when storing pine cones or other seeds. Vents near floor level ensure a supply of fresh air. The specification for thermal insulation and heating in the winter did not require living-room temperatures in the hall area. Radiators in the production area guarantee a minimum temperature and prevent condensation forming on the glass. The offices and laboratories in the two internal blocks are equipped with their own heating systems. This climate concept meant that insulating glass was not necessary. The U value of the laminated safety glass chosen is 5.6 W/m²K.

83

Detail of glazing at base. Size of panes: 972 x 528 mm to 982 x 1021 mm.

The layers of the frame structure.

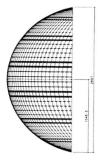

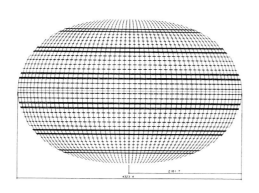

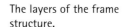

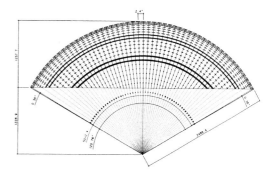

Section, scale 1:365.

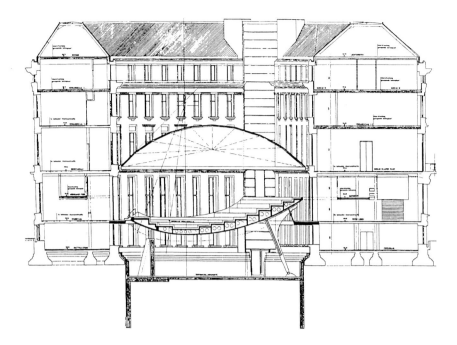

Plan of upper floor,
scale 1:730.

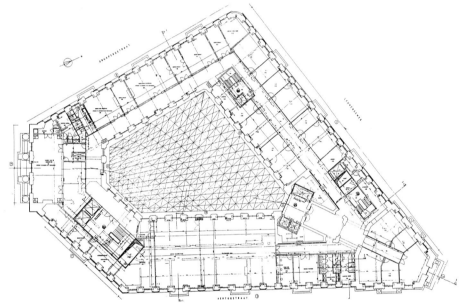

Isometric view of lattice
structure to steel–and–glass
dome with detail of node
point.

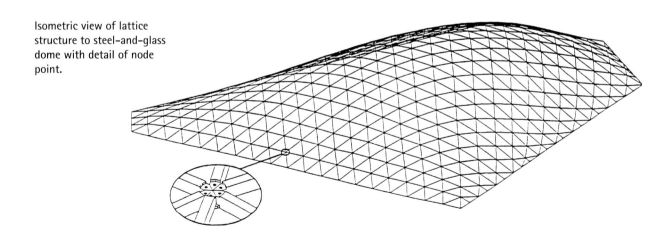

The glazed dome takes the plan form of the inner courtyard. It is supported on a lattice structure with intersecting members. The triangular, double-glazed insulating glass units consist of an outer pane of laminated safety glass (6 mm solar-control glass outer pane, 6 mm float glass inner pane, bonded with casting resin for sound insulation – both panes are toughened). The inner pane is made of laminated safety glass (2 x 4 mm float glass). Two smoke vents each with six flaps are incorporated at the crown.

Parliament of Flanders, Brussels
W. Verstraete, J. Puyen

On 17 February 1994 King Albert II of Belgium signed the new constitution which would turn his country into a confederation. From now on there would be three regions: Flanders, Wallonia and Brussels. In terms of language, Belgium comprises four groups: the French-speaking Walloons, the Flemish-speaking Flemings, the bilingual region of Brussels and a small German-speaking part. The elections of 21 May 1995 – a historic day in the 165-year history of the Kingdom of Belgium – saw 118 members of parliament directly elected to the *Vlaamse Raad*, the parliament of Flanders. Six Flemish MPs from the parliament of the Brussels region also have a seat in the *Vlaamse Raad*, bringing the total to 124. An existing administration building in Brussels, the capital of Flanders, became the new headquarters of the *Vlaamse Raad*. The plenary hall was incorporated underneath a glass roof in the inner courtyard of this block, which dates from the turn of the century.

New glass dome
The surface of this steel-and-glass dome is formed by stretching a membrane over the clear plan opening of the courtyard (analogous with a soap bubble). Loads placed on this membrane produce natural and harmonic deformations. After the plan has been divided up into vertical groups of areas like rows and columns, the intersections with the surface of the membrane can be used as points in space for the structural design of the members. These calculations for the members involved generating seven angles and three lengths for each of the 1200-plus members. Therefore, every member is unique, machined individually in one clamping on a computer-controlled machine specially set up for the purpose and working to an accuracy of a few-hundredths of a millimetre.

Glazing to curved surfaces
Node points in the form of two members crossing at right-angles or oblique angles are well known. Glass panes fixed to such a supporting structure are squares, diamonds or rectangles in plan. With planar supporting structures or glazed surfaces or supporting constructions only curved in one direction, no constructional difficulties arise; the individual panes of glass can be supported on and fixed to the sup-

Location
Der Vlaamse Raad, Leuwense-weg/rue de Louvain 27,
1000 Brussels, Belgium

Client
Der Vlaamse Raad, Brussels

Architects
Arrow, W. Verstraete, Gent
J. Puyen, Antwerp

Structural engineering and glass roof construction
Helmut Fischer GmbH, Talheim, Germany

Date of completion
1996

Entrance in existing building on the rue de Louvain/ Leuwenseweg.

Glass butt joint.

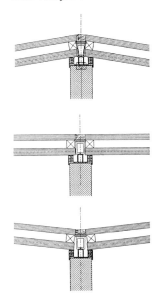

porting structure curved about one plane and butt-jointed at the appropriate angles. However, the problems come with glazed surfaces curved in two planes because then the corners of the panes, in themselves planar, cannot rest on all four node points simultaneously.

Lattice structure

Based on this state of the art technology, the task here was to glaze a large area over a supporting structure curved in three dimensions. Taking known connection designs, at which in each case more than four members can be joined by means of a screwed bracket, the new intersection is characterized by the fact that the ends of the members are pressed against each other over the area of at least one end face in each case and screwed together at their ends – and hence in the proximity of the node point – between two splice plates. In this type of connection, the compressive forces are transferred by contact between the end faces of the butt-jointed members, and tension via the splice plates on both sides of the joint, screwed together and covering the joint. Bending forces can also be easily accommodated. Therefore, the component tensile and compressive forces which ensue upon breaking down a bending moment can be transferred in the aforementioned manner either via one of the splice plates in the case of tension, or via the ends of several butted members in the case of compression.

Tapering the ends of members meeting at a node is advantageous; the end faces of adjoining members then butt together. This guarantees a good transfer of compressive forces and also allows the framework to be constructed in such a way that the nodes enclose triangular areas, permitting the use of triangular panes of glass. A structural member is then located along each edge of every pane. Therefore, surfaces curved in any direction can be formed and glazed. To meet the requirements, the angles between adjacent members are preferably between 0° and 180°; angles of 30-80° have proved sensible. With this arrangement, the loads to be carried can still be properly transferred to the other members meeting at the joint.

Detail of smoke vent: section, scale 1:5.

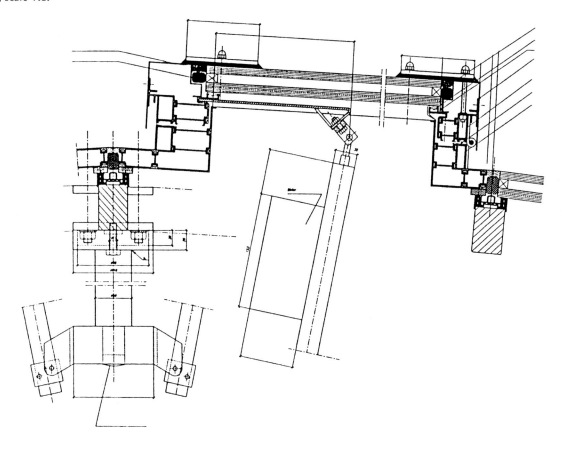

To keep the depth of the supporting construction to a minimum, both splice plates should be recessed a little into the ends of the members. This prevents the heads of the splice plate screws from colliding with the glass panes above which cover members and node points.

Ends of members can meet at any angle at a node point. Therefore, most of the connections in such a supporting structure will be one-offs, unique in that structure. Consequently, the demands placed on these joints are extremely high and the amount of work involved can only be handled by CAD methods. In order to be able to convert the computer's grid lines into a node-point grid correctly and simply, it is preferable to arrange the grid lines in the centre of the upper surface of the individual members. These grid lines then intersect at one point for each and every node. The intersection is then projected "downwards" from this theoretical node point. In order to do justice to the structural requirements, the splice plates are recessed into the ends of the members so that a predefined clearance always exists. As the splice plates also exhibit a constant thickness and shape for every node, comparable requirements can be established for the computation of all nodes.

The glazing over such a supporting structure can consist of single glazing, laminated safety glass made from several panes, or insulating glass units. One method of glazing a lattice structure which satisfies all technical requirements and has proved simple in terms of construction is the addition of a cover disc clamped from the outside onto the upper splice plate. Hence, the edges of the glass pane are clamped between two discs near the node point. One of the discs is the cover disc necessary for forming the connection; the other is additional and is easily screwed to the outer splice plate. The need to gain special approval for the lattice structure of this dome was unnecessary because the steelwork complies with the regulations.

Glazing

The dome is covered with double-glazed insulating glass units which provide solar-control and acoustic insulation properties. The outer pane of the unit is 6 mm solar-control, laminated safety glass ("Cool-Lite" SS 120) and the inner pane 6 mm float glass. To achieve good sound insulation, the panes are bonded together with catalyst-cured resin (±1 mm thick). Both panes are toughened and the cavity is 15 mm. The inner pane of the unit consists of two 4 mm panes of laminated safety glass (float glass). The light transmittance of the glazing is 18%, the U value 2.26 W/m²K. Smoke vents are incorporated at the crown of the dome.

Plenary hall in inner court-yard under the glass dome with solar-control and sound insulating glass.

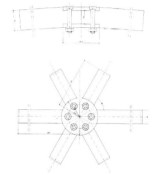

Hexagonal node point with contact between ends of compression members. A patent has been applied for.

Detail of smoke vent: plan and section (right), scale 1:25.

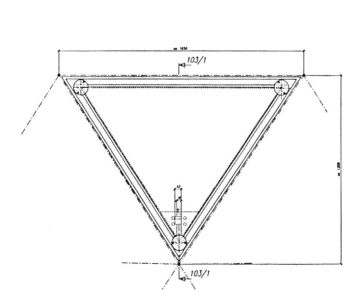

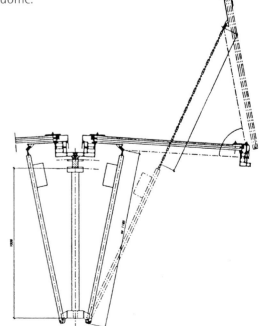

Isometric view.

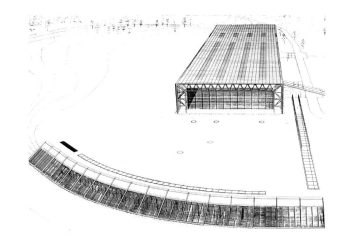

Site plan.

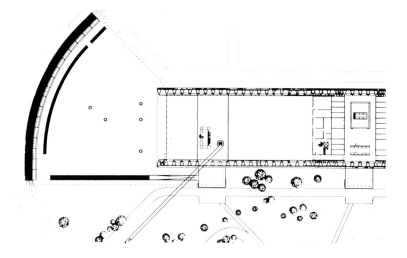

Section.

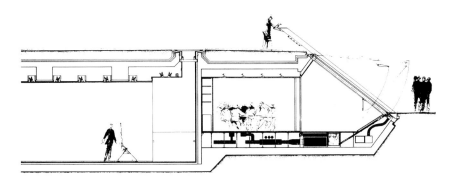

Ground floor.

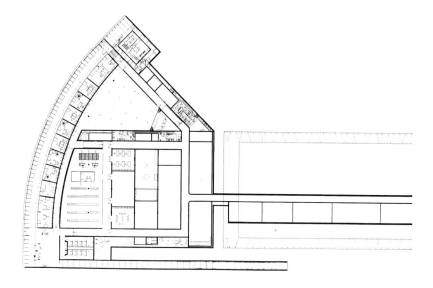

Sainsbury Centre – Crescent Wing, Norwich
Sir Norman Foster

The Sainsbury Centre for Visual Art was built in 1974-78 for the art collection of Sir Robert and Lady Sainsbury on the Campus of the University of East Anglia. Besides housing the collection, it offers a range of facilities for public and acedemic uses beneath a large-span roof. Sir Norman Foster was awarded the 1979 Reynolds Memorial Award for his design. By 1979 an extension had become necessary and so the architects added the new "Crescent Wing" – so named because of its shape – below ground on the eastern side. The inclined glazing of the new addition is arranged in a broad arc facing onto a wide valley containing a man-made lake. Access to the wing is via a ramp which begins next to the entrance to the main building and leads downwards beneath a glass roof. The arc of the corridor meets the entrance to the subterranean wing beneath the inclined glazing. There is further glazing on the corridor side of the adjacent study rooms. The storeroom for the collection, accessible to visitors, is located in Crescent Wing, where the exhibits are now housed in glass display cabinets and a glazed archive store with mobile shelving units that are moved apart for access. This advanced storage system was designed by George Saxton Associates, who also designed the facilities for the Henry R. Luce Study Centre in the Metropolitan Museum of Art in New York. The restorers' rooms are situated in the centre of the wing. Adding the lower gallery means that the Sainsbury Centre now has 700 m² of floor space available for non-permanent exhibitions. This area can also be used as a lecture hall for up to 200 people. Lighting arrangements within the gallery are such that it can also be used as a room for experimenting with museum lighting. A back-projection system is installed on the end wall for audio-visual presentations.

Glass elements
Glass had already featured prominently in the design for the main hall of the Sainsbury Centre. Fully glazed walls comprising 12 laminated safety glass panes, each 2.4 x 7.5 m and 15 mm thick, form each of the gable ends. At the butt joints, glass stiffeners guarantee the glass walls the necessary stability. In the case of Crescent Wing, glass was again employed as a primary element in the layout and lighting of the underground facilities. The entrance via the downward ramp is ar-

Location
University of East Anglia, Norwich, UK

Client
University of East Anglia

Architects
Sir Norman Foster & Partners, London

Project team
Chubby Chhabra, Chris Connell, Sir Norman Foster, Richard Hawkins, Heiko Lukas, Graham Phillips

Museum and lighting consultant
George Sexton Associates, Washington DC

Glas construction
MBM Metallbau Möckmühl GmbH

Printed glass
BGT Bischoff Glastechnik GmbH, Bretten

Date of completion
1991

The inclined glazing in front of the outer corridor.

The panes of insulating glass making up the inclined glazing in front of the outer corridor are printed with a pattern of white dots, the density of which gradually increases towards the top of the panes.

Escape doors open upwards.

A strip of non-slip laminated safety glass in the lawn serves as rooflight.

The internal corridor is lit by a strip of roof light.

ranged in such a way that the visitor's view is directed towards the landscape while descending the ramp. The first section of the glass covering the ramp is a raised hood glazed on three sides, with no fall to the roof. The second section is at ground level, embedded in the lawns. This glazing can withstand pedestrian traffic. The laminated safety glass panes have a non-slip, translucent, silk-screen ceramic ink coating which is baked on. Again, this roof has no fall.

Inclined glazing

Crescent Wing is located on a sort of terrace within the terrain. At the transition to the meadow at a lower level, the extension is in the shape of an arc which opens up towards the surrounding countryside via inclined glazing. The insulating glass employed here is printed with a pattern of white dots which becomes gradually denser as it rises in order to provide privacy and shading from the sun. The density of the printing progresses from 2% to 97% over a length of 4.3 m. At eye level, the printing is still sufficiently transparent, while at the top of the panes it offers shade against the sun. Another effect of this printing is that the curve of the windows does not appear as a dark band during the day, which would be the case with unprinted glass. Vision is hardly impaired by the pattern of dots. The inclined façade includes escape doors which open upwards.

Overhead lighting

The internal corridor, which follows the outer curve on the rear side of the study rooms, is lit by a strip of rooflights made from non-slip, laminated safety glass fixed flush with the lawns over the extension. This ensures a particularly bright, vertical light from above which, owing to a grid attached beneath the glass, is distributed in a diffuse fashion and reflected from the white walls.

Sculptures behind safety glass in the storeroom.

91

Entrance ramp leading down to Crescent Wing.

The view from the ramp towards the upper entrance in the vicinity of the raised glass roof.

Plan, 1st floor,
scale 1:500.

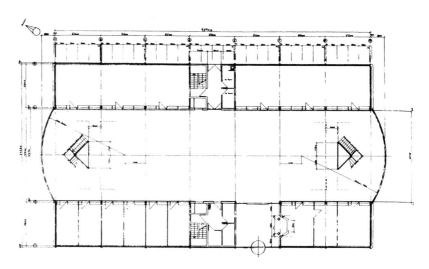

Plan, ground floor,
scale 1:500.

Vertical section through
window in structural glazing
façade.

Vertical section through in-
situ construction to structural glazing façade.

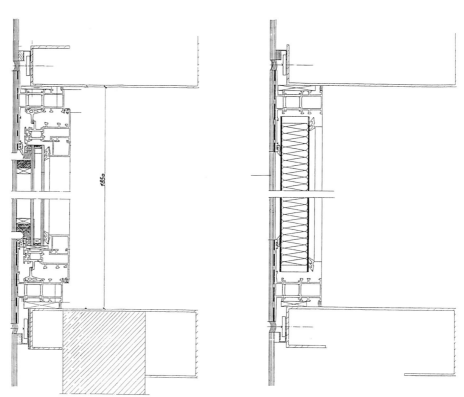

Office building, H. Fischer, Talheim
Art & Design

In the roughly 40 years of its existence, the metal fabrication firm of Helmut Fischer GmbH has built up a reputation throughout Europe in the field of glass roofs and glass façades. By the early 1990s, the company had outgrown its premises and expansion in the form of a new office building was urgently required. Following the purchase of an adjoining plot of land, the directors of the company decided to erect a new building. There was a wish and indeed a self-imposed obligation to find challenging solutions in terms of construction and design, above all in the field of glass construction.

The general concept provided for a three-storey building with parking below in a semi-basement. The large glass atrium in the centre was to be flanked by two office wings. Therefore, staff have to pass through the atrium, turning it into a central communication zone. The size of the atrium was dictated by the specification, which called for an area capable of accommodating works meetings, Christmas parties and similar events. This area can also be used for cultural purposes, e.g. exhibitions and concerts.

Steelwork was chosen for the building in conjunction with in-situ works in which the spandrel panels act as loadbearing elements for the intermediate floors. Permanent formwork was employed which helps to carry the loads and forms cable ducts internally.

Glass construction

In line with the desire for flat glazing in one plane for the elevations, a structural glazing solution was chosen. The glass construction, designed by the Fischer company itself, was based on "Wicona" profiled sections, series No. L-70 A. For ventilation purposes, conventional window openings were included in the glass façade in the form of tilt or tilt-and-turn windows. The glass atrium was given a lattice-type vaulted roof and the gable ends to the atrium treated similarly. The glazing to the roof consists of insulating glass units with outer panes of body-tinted grey "Parsol" float glass, 8 mm thick, a 12 mm cavity and inner panes of laminated safety glass, 10 mm thick, with a K-glass coating (Pilkington insulting glass, direct on-line pyrolytic coating).

Location
Helmut Fischer GmbH,
Im Eggerten 1-3,
74388 Talheim, Germany

Client
Helmut Fischer GmbH

Architects
Art & Design, Talheim/Flein

Site Manager
Peter Ohr, Heilbronn

Structural engineers
Schlaich, Bergermann &
Partner, Stuttgart

Date of completion
1992

The central area serves as a communication zone below the barrel-vault glass roof.

Details of the glass stairs: top, section through stair, scale 1:50; bottom centre, section through glass pane and supporting arm; details of connections.

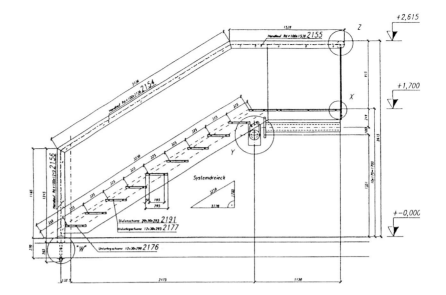

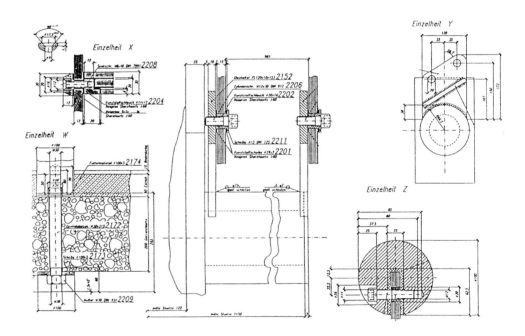

Horizontal section through structural glazing façade.
1 Tilt-and-turn window.
2 Insulating glass: inside, 6 mm float glass, 12 mm cavity between panes.
3 Toughened safety glass, grey, 6 mm, outside.

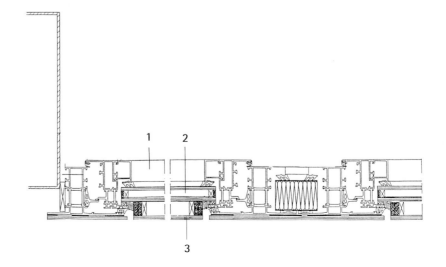

Main entrance in the reflective structural glazing façade beneath a suspended glass roof of laminated safety glass with individual bolted fixings.

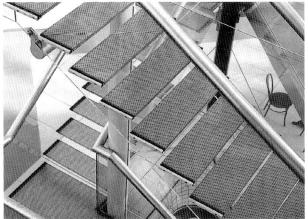 

The glazed stair stringers made from laminated safety glass are suspended from the solid stainless steel handrails. A non-slip, printed pattern is baked onto the laminated safety glass treads.

The triangular stairwell is glazed and serves as a ventilation shaft.

Lighting in the atrium is provided by 1250 light bulbs each of 15 W attached to the barrel-vault glass roof, connected within the profiled sections by 1.2 km of cable! A 45-m-long vent is incorporated at the crown for ventilation and as a smoke outlet. This continuous ribbon of glass is raised evenly by means of 34 hydraulic cylinders, resulting in a clear opening of 27.5 m^2 for ventilation or to allow smoke to escape in case of fire. Tilting windows at the base of the vertical glazing serve to admit fresh air. Hence, natural convection currents are set up which ensure eight air-changes per hour.

Glass stairs and bridges

At both gable ends, bridges incorporating glass elements link the office wings on both sides of the atrium. These are in turn linked to the floor of the atrium via glass stairs. The triangular stairwells are glazed and serve as ventilation shafts in which the warm atrium air is drawn downwards from above. A heating battery then heats up this air before it is blown out into the body of the atrium again. The stairs themselves, made completely from glass, have solid stainless steel handrails from which the stair stringers are suspended. These glass stair structures have demonstrated their design quality in over five years of continuous usage.

The glass stairs, landings and walkways are composed of the following types of glass

Stair stringers
12 mm laminated safety glass, heat-treated.

Stair treads
3-ply laminated safety glass, total thickness approx. 31 mm, with non-slip, silk-screen colour coating, PVB interlayers, each 2.28 mm; glass: top – 8 mm toughened safety glass, middle – 10 mm heat-treated glass, bottom – 8 mm heat-treated glass.

Walkways
3-ply laminated safety glass, total thickness approx. 33 mm with non-slip, silk-screen colour printing; glass: top – 8 mm toughened safety glass, middle – 12 mm heat-treated glass, bottom – 8 mm heat-treated glass.

Plans, ground floor, standard floor, conference floor, rooftop terrace, scale 1:800.

97

RWE Tower, Essen
Ingenhoven, Overdiek + Partner

The RWE Tower is situated near the main station in Essen, opposite the Stadtgarten Park and the Aalto Theatre. A public forecourt covered by a high-level canopy links the gardens within the block with the park. With 30 storeys totalling 120 m, plus another 7 m for the external lifts tower and its 35 m aerial, the 162 m overall height of the RWE Tower is the highest point in the Ruhr district. The building is erected over a circular plan, 32 m in diameter. It stands on a single-storey plinth, one façade of which is provided with "cockpit-like" inclined glazing offering a view of the park and lake. This allows generous daylighting of conference zone, restaurant and recreation rooms. Above this level, the entrance hall occupies the entire ground floor apart from the shafts for stairs, services and fire brigade lifts, one set on each side. The offices on the upper floors all have an unobstructed view to the outside and are all accessed from a circular corridor. The inner core areas receive daylight by way of overhead glazing. The top five floors are connected via an atrium and internal stairs. The conference room on the top floor gains additional illumination through a rooflight, above which there is a steel framework with louvres.

Ground floor façade

The 8.4-m-high entrance hall is glazed full height with "Climaplus N" extra-clear insulating glass panes arranged in pairs – each 4.2 m high. The build-up of these insulating glass units is as follows: 10 mm toughened safety glass, 19 mm cavity and 17 mm laminated safety glass consisting of toughened safety glass. They are held in place by individual bolted fixings on internal aluminium sections. These sections incorporate fresh-air channels with nozzles to expel the air. A one-piece, internal sunshade and antiglare screen has been installed, 8 m high, powered by electric motors and controlled via the building management system according to the respective ambient conditions.

Location
RWE AG, Konzernzentrale
Essen, Am Aalto Theater,
45128 Essen, Germany

Client
Hochtief AG, Essen

Architects
Ingenhoven Overdiek Kahlen
und Partner, Düsseldorf

Project team
Christoph Ingenhoven, Achim
Nagel, Klaus Frankenheim,
Klaus J. Osterburg, Martin
Slawik, Elisabeth Viera, Peter-
Jan van Owerkerk, Imre Halmai,
Claudia de Bruyn, Jan Dvorak,
Norbert Siepmann, Regina
Wulff, Martin Döring

Façade design
Josef Gartner & Co.,
Gundelfingen

Date of completion
1996

North elevation.

Section along entrance axis.
At first basement level is the
"cockpit" façade; above the
17th floor the 7-m-high
plant hall.

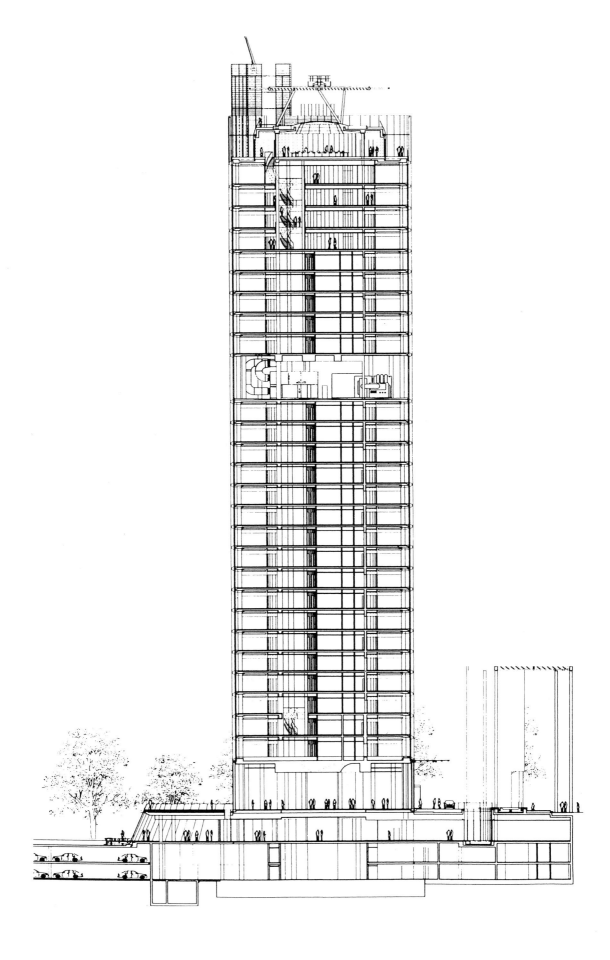

"Cockpit" façade

The inclined cockpit façade at first basement level creates the link between the casino area and the park and lake on the side away from the road. The geometry of this façade corresponds to the development of a truncated cone. Realization of the complicated geometry – every pane and every section has a different format and different shape – was made possible by way of CAD and CAM methods. Non-coloured, solar-control insulating glass was used for the glazing. The internal supporting structure, employing sharp-edged sections, has an overall height of 4.9 m. A special feature of this façade are the three inclined, storey-height hinged doors extending across two bays, 4.0 m wide and 5.4 m high, which can be opened by means of electropneumatic rams. These allow access from the restaurant to the lakeside terrace. The glass used is intruder-resistant and, in some places, bullet-resistant.

Ventilation façade

The office floors of the tower have a double-skin glass façade. The smooth, fully glazed outer skin of extra clear, i.e. low iron oxide, toughened safety glass, 10 mm thick, encloses a conventional, thermally insulated inner skin. The outer glass façade is provided with ventilation openings to the outside through which air is drawn into and exhausted from the 500 mm cavity between the two skins. Protected from the weather, the cavity contains shading and antiglare louvre blinds comprising 80 mm aluminium strips, controlled centrally depending on the sun. In addition, they can be adjusted individually for each room. For thermal and acoustic reasons, the cavity is divided up horizontally at the level of the reinforced concrete floor slabs by means of ventilation ducts, and vertically at alternate grid lines (1970 mm grid dimension) by glazed bulkheads.

Inner skin

This skin is formed by a storey-height glass wall with aluminium framing and sections of glass which can be slid sideways by hand. The glass used is "Climaplus" extra clear insulating glass. By employing clear glass for both skins, the additive effect of the slight green tint of normal glass is avoided. Every bay has one fixed and one opening section, 912 x 3061 mm. The standard storey height is 3591 mm but it does vary (max. 3780 mm). The sliding sections can be opened a maximum of

Glazing on the rooftop terrace.

Glass dome over conference room. The sunshading installation can be seen above the dome.

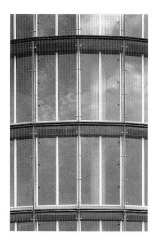

Part elevation of façade to offices area.

Model of "fish's mouth" cladding. Per storey, each pair of window bays is ventilated diagonally via "spoilers".

Façade section, typical floor.

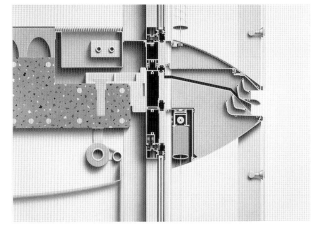
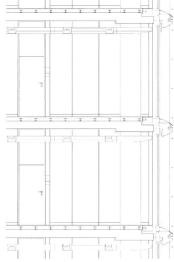

Installing a pre-assembled glass façade element.

135 mm for ventilation; however, they can be opened fully for maintenance and cleaning purposes, for which a special crank fitting was developed.

Outer skin
Each piece of the toughened safety glass which makes up the outer skin measures 1970 x 3461 mm and is held by eight bolted fixings. The 500 mm cavity of the façade is ventilated via a 150-mm-wide joint in the outer skin. Specially developed "spoilers" direct the fresh air into the "fish's mouth". The underside of this opening is formed by a solid plate whereas the top has a perforated one, alternately connected to the storeys above and below. Each pair of adjacent bays forms one unit, with one field having the vent at the top and the other at the bottom. This corresponds with the principle of diagonal through-ventilation developed for this project, a method which guarantees that no short-circuit currents of stale air can form between the individual floors.

Erecting the façade
The 7,000 m² of the double-skin façade construction comprises 962 storey-height elements measuring 1970 x 3591 mm or 1970 x 3780 mm. They were factory-assembled into units, with all the components of the inner and outer skins already integrated, prior to transport to the site. Upon arrival, they were fitted directly to the fixing brackets already in position.

Plant hall

A 7-m-high plant hall forms the 18th storey. As, initially, it could not be ruled out that during unfavourable weather conditions moisture in the outgoing air might condense on cold parts of the façade at this level and cause the formation of icicles, which could be dangerous if they fell, the contractors and designers instigated an experiment. This involved wind tunnel tests and a theoretical study with simulation calculations. The solution proved to be a continuous outer skin of toughened safety glass (clear) – a total of 600 m² – with individual bolted fixings, and an inner skin of aluminium louvres and integral air nozzles, 900 mm dia. The aluminium nozzles extend to the outer skin in order to draw in fresh air from outside. These nozzles help to give the outgoing air sufficient momentum to eject it clear of the immediate proximity of the building so that it mixes with dry outside air. The exit velocity and direction are carefully varied depending on the speed and direction of the wind around the building as well as the outside temperature. This is done in order to reduce the power required for the fans and minimize the noise level of the exhaust nozzles so as not to disturb the occupants unduly.

Thermal, acoustic and internal–climate aspects

A whole series of criteria had to be investigated during the development of the double-skin façade. To accomplish this, wind tunnel tests were carried out on 1:500 and 1:64 models in order to determine and optimize the design. In addition, a specimen 1:1 façade section with a room behind was built and tested under natural, external conditions, with the experiments being backed up by theoretical studies. The work revealed that sunshading in the cavity is equal to that of an external blind. An interesting self-regulation effect also came to light, which was later quantified through measurements. It was demonstrated that the air-change rate in the cavity also rose as the solar radiation increased. The heating up of the components of the façade – glass, framing and sunshading – also heats up the boundary layer of the currents of air around the building and creates a convection effect. The

Office with full-height glazing.

Upper junction in double-skin façade.

Storey-height hinged glass
door extending over two
bays, 4.0 m wide, 5.4 m
high.

Section, hinged door in
"cockpit" façade,
scale 1:200.

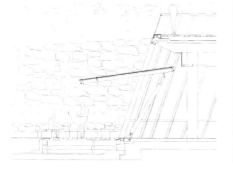

hotter the façade in comparison to the surrounding air, the more noticeable is this
convection and the more pronounced is the air circulation within the cavity. Therefore, the surfaces of the blinds dissipate more heat energy and the sunshading
functions better as the solar radiation increases.

The "sick-building syndrome" found in air-conditioned buildings can often be
traced back to a lack of ventilation via open windows. For this reason, the tower
should be able to be ventilated for as long a period as possible. The most crucial
requirement for this is an effective reduction of the wind pressure on the façade.
Therefore, a lengthy optimization process led to the baffles in the fish's mouths
being designed in such a way that the drop in pressure in the façade when the
windows are open, more or less irrespective of the external wind conditions, leads
to optimum air-change rates and pressures in the cavity. Dr Heusler from Gartner,
responsible for the façade design, commented on this aspect: "From time to time,
suspicions are expressed among experts that at higher windspeeds high-rise buildings with double-skin façades and opening windows can lead to draughts inside
the building and internal doors needing unreasonable force to open them. The
results of the investigations into façade, storey and building through-ventilation
initiated for this very reason show that a 28-m-high building with a conventional
façade on the edge of a built-up area – a situation for which we have had much
practical data for many years –, the effort needed to open a door can be expected
to be 20% higher than at a height of 88 m in the RWE Tower with its double-skin
façade. Comparing the through-currents of the two buildings leads to an even
more marked difference. In the 28 m building, the internal air velocities are
2.5 times those of our glass cylinder and so lead us to expect draughts twice as
often as in the RWE building. To sum up, it can be established that in this case the
ventilation plant can be switched off for nearly 70% of the year. During the rest of
the year, increased ventilation heat losses, low air humidity, unacceptably high

"Cockpit" façade in basement storey in front of the casino area.

Entrance. There are 336 solar panels on the roof of the projecting high-level canopy at a height of 25 m. These achieve 19 kW$_p$ maximum rated output under standard test conditions.

internal temperatures, draughts or insufficient air changes would ensue with unfavourable weather conditions. The appropriate sensors attached to the building plus a master computer and windows fitted with signalling devices can be used to inform the occupants whether it really is advisable to open windows during the weather conditions (wind, rain, hot, cold) prevailing at that moment. When occupants are advised against opening windows, then a mechanical ventilation plant with heat recovery ensures a supply of fresh air." The double-skin façade is also distinguished by a higher utilization of passive solar energy. This is due to the cavity, which acts like a greenhouse. The superimposition of reduced transmission and ventilation heat losses allows the heating energy requirement to be roughly halved with respect to a conventional façade equal in standard to the inner skin in this case.

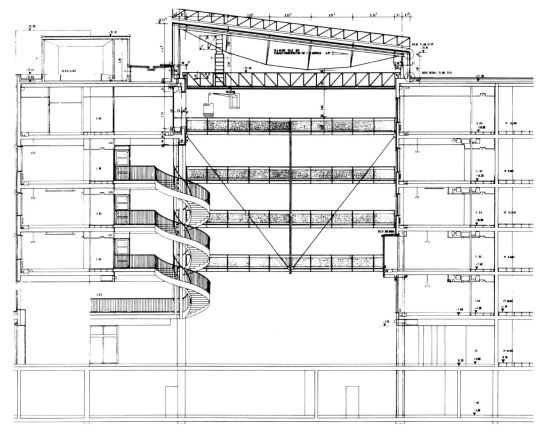

Section through atrium, scale 1:300.

Plans of garden level and ground floor.

Opposite page:

Main entrance with glass canopy.

Minimal steelwork on the glass gable wall and glass monopitch roof. The maximum length of the roof is 59 m and the width 18.5 m.

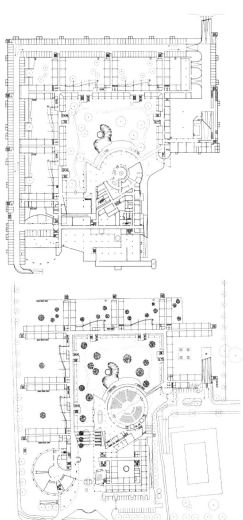

Telekom Headquarters, Bonn
Kammerer + Belz, Kucher and Partner

The location of the plot on Friedrich-Ebert-Allee presented a difficult situation. The neighbouring buildings on this busy road are three important museums: the History Museum of the Federal Republic of Germany, the Bonn Art Museum and the Art and Exhibition Hall of the Federal Republic of Germany. In addition, ministries, party headquarters, embassies and hotels line up along this road linking Bonn with Bad Godesberg. As building height is restricted here, no high-rise tower was possible. Therefore, Deutsche Telekom AG had to find a low-rise solution to house the 2,000 staff who work at the group's head office. The 50,000 m^2 plot is roughly square. A projecting corner leads via a gently curving line to the great glazed atrium. Inside, wide steps lead down to a 5000 m^2 sunken garden, bounded on three sides by long office blocks. The office wings spread out like fingers – three to the south, three to the east and two to the north – from the garden. Most of the offices are housed here, with natural ventilation and daylighting. The offices, 16.2 m^2 on average, have windows which look out either onto the central garden or to outer courtyards. Two large, round structures, offset diagonally, are placed to the left and right of the atrium. The left-hand block contains a large conference zone at ground floor level and, above, the library. The right-hand block houses an 800-seat hall, which can be divided to make smaller units, and, below, the restaurant seating 330, linked to the sunken garden.

Glass-and-steel construction

The heart of this complex – the great glass atrium – is characterized by the minimal amount of steelwork used for the glazed sections, lending the atrium maximum transparency. These sections comprise the monopitch roof, the gable walls to the north and south, and the ridge and eaves walls running along the length of the atrium. The glazing bars are taken as loadbearing components in all the sections of

Location
Generaldirektion Telekom AG,
Friedrich-Ebert-Allee,
53113 Bonn, Germany

Client
GENIUS
Grundstückverwaltungsgesellschaft,
Munich

Planners and architects
Kammerer + Belz, Kucher and
Partner, Stuttgart
Prof. Walter Belz and Dipl.-Ing.
Klaus Kucher

Partners
Josef Greitzke, Alfons Hahn,
Wolfgang Lutz, Ulrich Ziegler

Project Manager
Alfons Hahn

Project management
Drees & Sommer, Stuttgart

Design of glass construction
Robert Danz, Schönaich

Manufacture and erection of
glass construction
Josef Gartner & Co.,
Gundelfingen

Date of completion
1995

Glass façade in entrance area, scale 1:100. "Infrastop Neutral 51/38" solar-control insulating glass. At ground and 1st floor levels, the outer panes are 10 mm toughened safety glass and the inner panes "Allstop Privat A 3" laminated safety glass, with a 12 mm cavity. At the higher levels, two panes of float glass, 19 mm thick, 12 mm cavity.

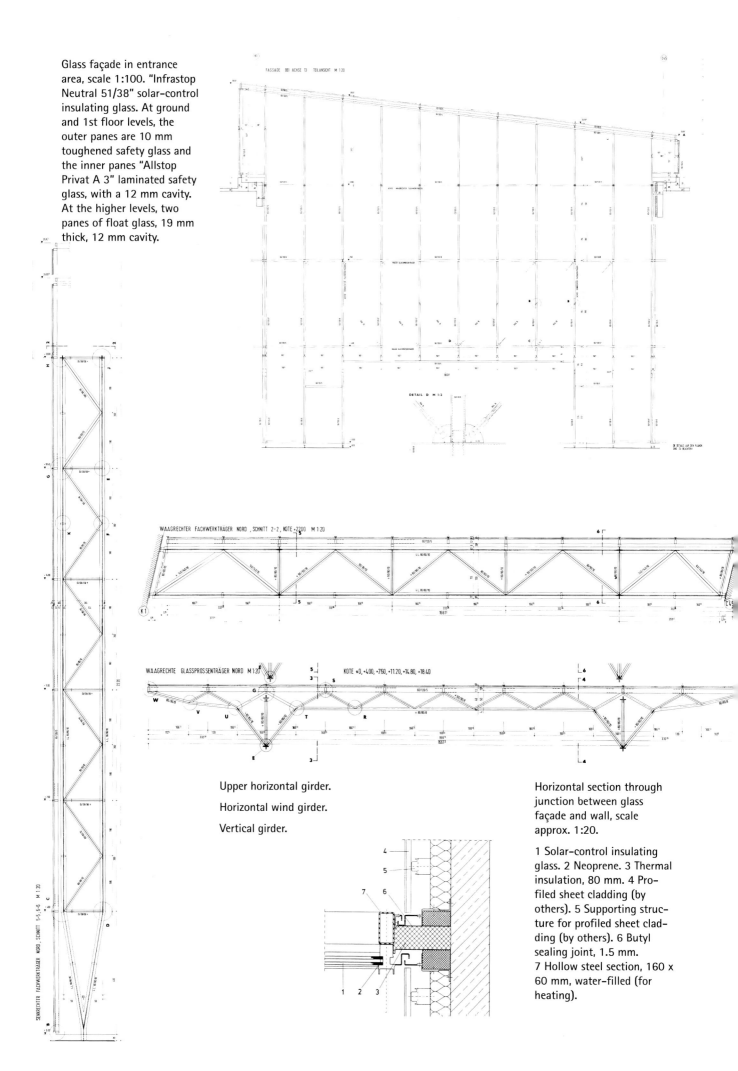

Upper horizontal girder.

Horizontal wind girder.

Vertical girder.

Horizontal section through junction between glass façade and wall, scale approx. 1:20.

1 Solar-control insulating glass. 2 Neoprene. 3 Thermal insulation, 80 mm. 4 Profiled sheet cladding (by others). 5 Supporting structure for profiled sheet cladding (by others). 6 Butyl sealing joint, 1.5 mm. 7 Hollow steel section, 160 x 60 mm, water-filled (for heating).

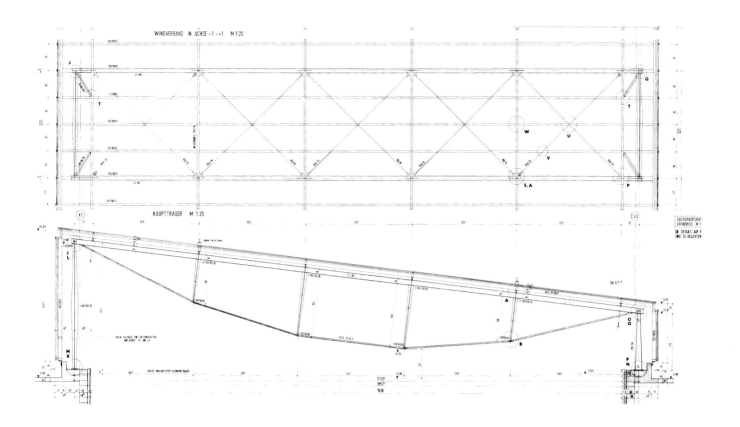

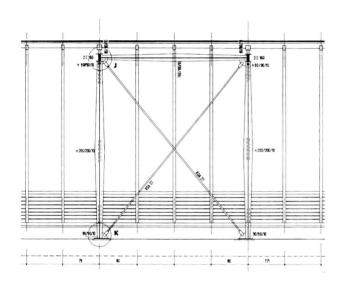

Plan of part of glass roof.

Trussed main beam.

Elevation on glass wall and longitudinal bracing below roof support.

Detail H of base of girder, scale 1:10.

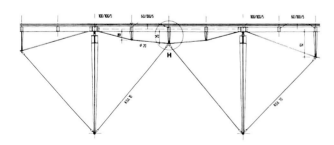

Trussed purlin adjacent the longitudinal bracing.

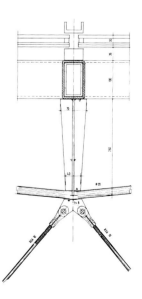

Wide steps lead to the
central garden.

Vertical girders on the gable.

the roof and wall construction. They form the compression chords of the trussed beams. Further, the glazing bars are water-filled for heating the façades and roof (Gartner Integrated Façade System). The two high gable walls (max. height 30.5 m, width of main façade 17.05 m) are supported by two vertical girders, 1580 mm deep and 9.675 m apart, and one horizontal girder, 1580 mm deep and positioned at +21.75 m level. Behind every horizontal glazing bar – at 3.55 m centres – there is a 500-mm-deep girder which transfers the wind loads to the two vertical girders. The girders consist of sharp-edged cruciform steel sections, 80 x 80 x 8 mm, and 80 x 80 x 10 mm angles.

In the entrance zone, the vertical glazing bars are held by a storey-height girder. The columns and beams of the façade change to girders at this point, with additional axial ties included as diagonals extending over two bays. The circular entrance lobby, 9.3 m dia., is positioned beneath the ensuing portal.

The glass roof, max. width 18.5 m and max. length 59 m, is supported on glass walls along the two longitudinal sides of the atrium. The monopitch roof, 6.75% slope, is supported by underslung trusses at 6.2 m centres. The glazing bars, 60 x 100 x 5 mm square hollow sections, are designed as trussed beams in the longitudinal axis. Aluminium, motorized vents are incorporated in the longitudinal façade of the roof and in the gables. The atrium is glazed with "Infrastop Neutral" solar-control insulating glass units. These units comprise an outer pane of 8 mm toughened safety glass, a 12 mm cavity and an inner pane of 10 mm laminated safety glass. The g-value of the glass is 51%, the U value 1.6 W/m^{2}K. The surfaces of the steelwork were given a coat of two-component clear polyurethane micaceous iron-ore paint. The external, cold-formed aluminium bars were powder-coated. The patented Rodan system was used for all ties.

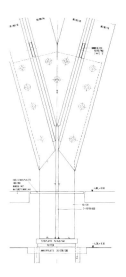

Detail of base of vertical girder.

Plan, ground floor,
scale 1:500.

Plan, upper floor,
scale 1:500.

Isometric view of façade
construction.

Right: Entrance elevation.
The façade of frosted laminated safety glass leads the
viewer to surmise the interior.

Corner detail of "shingle-
like" glass façade. The panes
of laminated safety glass are
inclined both vertically and
horizontally and are held in
place by separate chromium
steel castings.

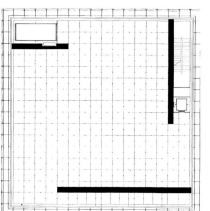

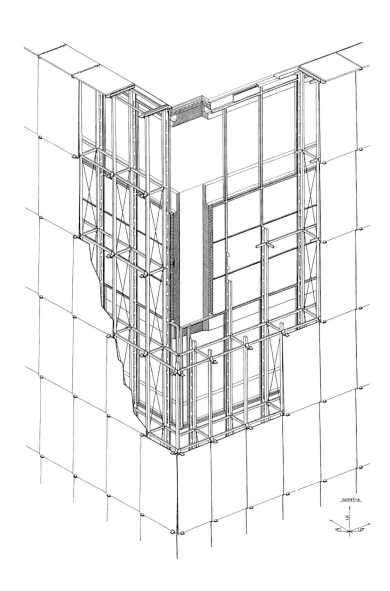

Art gallery, Bregenz
Peter Zumthor

In keeping with its location in Bregenz on the shores of Lake Constance, where three countries meet – Germany, Austria, Switzerland –, the concept of this art gallery and its exhibition programme strives for an international flavour in its treatment of contemporary art. Under the title "Archive – Art – Architecture", the transitional domains of contemporary art and architecture form a special thematic focus. Up to 10 exhibitions per year are envisaged, organized primarily by the gallery itself. The architect Peter Zumthor has given the building its very own distinctive character through the design, the materials and the interplay with light. It is the first significant new building in Austria devoted to contemporary art since the Vienna Secessionists almost 100 years previously. The glazed block, 26.57 x 26.57 x 30 m high, stands on the lakeside promenade between the post office and the theatre. Its external appearance is distinguished by façades of frosted (acid-embossed) panes of glass arranged like scales which reflect daylight and are lit from inside in the evenings. The 1989 competition-winning design was built in 1994-97. Three transverse shear walls form the internal structure of this square building which houses the exhibitions on the three upper floors above the entrance and foyer at ground floor level. The two basement levels contain a lecture room, the gallery's teaching department, stores, workshops and toilets. Together with the gallery administration – a separate building containing offices, cafeteria and gallery shop –, the art gallery forms a square between a bay on the lake and the old quarter of the town.

Building envelope

Steelwork consisting of hollow steel sections surrounds the in-situ construction of the exhibition building itself. The posts are 100 x 60 mm hollow steel sections with various wall thicknesses, and the beams 60 x 40 x 4 mm hollow sections. A total of 712 panes of laminated safety glass, comprising two 10 mm panes of extra-clear float glass with a 4-ply interlayer and a frosted outer surface, form the external,

Location
Kunsthaus Bregenz,
Karl-Tizian-Platz,
6900 Bregenz, Austria

Client
State of Vorarlberg

Architect
Peter Zumthor, Haldenstein

Project Manager
Daniel Bosshard

Site supervision
Feldkirch Building Dept, Martin
Zerlauth, Kornelia Rhomberg,
Othmar Huber

Structural engineers
Robert Manahl, Bregenz

Structural glazing
Ernst Wälchli, Langenthal,
Dr Rudolf Hess, ETH Zürich

Energy concept
Meierhans & Partner, Zürich

Façades
feroplan engineering, Chur

Glass construction
Glas Marte GmbH, Bregenz

Date of completion
1997

ventilated envelope. These panes, each 1.72 x 2.93 m and weighing 252 kg, are inclined in both the horizontal and vertical planes, like shingle cladding. Brackets made from chromium steel castings – two at the top, two at the bottom – hold each of the panes in place. Thick-walled silicone profiles are factory-glued to the bearing points. The upper silicone pieces, in combination with small glass plates glued on and a projecting fin, form a slit in the rear of the bracket, by way of which the glass is considerably delayed from dropping out of the upper fixing if the pane is severely damaged. This adhesive joint needed special care during production as it forms a loadbearing connection if the glass is broken. Therefore, every 15th glued joint was tested during production, and the tests supervised by an officially authorized materials testing institute.

The internal glazing consists of insulating glass. At ground and first floor, the glass comprises an inner pane of laminated safety glass (two 6 mm panes of float glass), a 12 mm krypton-filled cavity and a 6 mm float glass outer pane. The U value is 1.1 W/m^2K. The strips of rooflights and the top two floors employ insulating glass with extra-clear 6 mm float glass for the inner pane, a 12 mm argon-filled cavity and an extra-clear 6 mm float glass outer pane. The U value is 1.3 W/m^2K. These insulating glass types also have a frosted finish.

Glass assembly of the internal façade

The erection of the glazing placed high demands on the contractor. For instance, the inner panes of the insulating glass could not be installed from inside because the units were much larger than the clear openings to be glazed. From outside was impossible too because the steelwork prevented access. The only solution was the method outlined in the tender documents: from the roof, with the insulating glass units being passed down a slot in the steel frame into their allotted positions.

The total area of insulating glass was 2000 m^2, and the largest units measured 1.42 x 4 m and weighed 255 kg. To install such an area properly, a travelling crane assembly for two travelling chain hoists was mounted on the roof. This enabled the glazing units to be lifted out of their transport containers and onto the roof, from where they were lowered up to 32 m through the erection slot – which only allowed 16 mm clearance between moving glass and rigid steel frame! To check the function of this special construction, a mock-up of the façade was tested in Glas Marte's works. As it could not be ruled out that the narrow slot might be made even narrower due to protruding bolts, a timber "dummy" was fabricated and fitted with a multitude of electrical contacts wired to an alarm. Before lowering the glass down a slot, the timber dummy was first inserted each time to check for possible problems. This enabled the demanding glazing to be accomplished on time.

Glass assembly of the external façade

The external glazing was also erected from the roof. A suspended cradle for the erectors was fitted to the crane. The crane lifted the glazing units onto the roof and then lowered them into position. The contact pressure of the setting-up angle was specified by the structural engineers and produced by a special construction with integral ring-force gauge. The reading was recorded for every single mounting. This construction was only made possible through the extensive calculations and time-consuming trials of the structural glass specialists Dr Rudolf Hess and Ernst Wälchli.

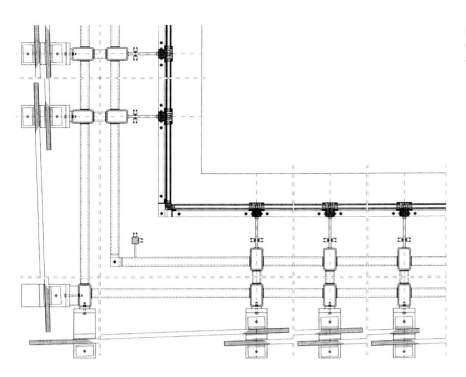

Horizontal section through overhead lighting level, scale approx. 1:25.

View through 2-m-deep suspended glass ceiling over exhibition room towards glazed external façade through which daylight enters above the non-loadbearing enclosing walls.

Fixing for glass "shingles".

The automated glazing assembly on the roof of the gallery. Using suction cups, it lifts the units out of their transport containers and moves them into the rail system for assembly.

The glass ceiling mounting specially developed by Glas Marte for this project.

Steelwork of façade with inner glazing installed.

"Threading" a 1.42 x 4 m insulating glass unit into the narrow erection slot.

Exhibition room beneath suspended glass ceiling of frosted laminated safety glass.

Vertical section through edge of roof, scale 1:25.

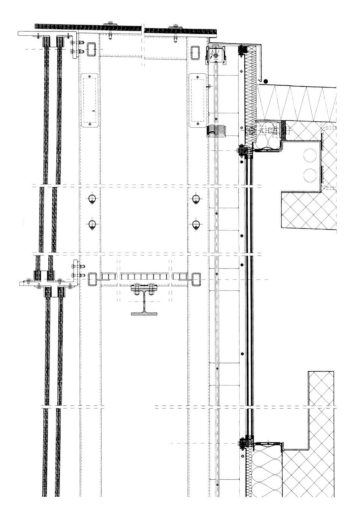

Glass ceilings

Daylight is directed into the exhibition rooms on the upper three floors via glass ceilings. These consist of square panes of glass attached by means of individual bolted fixings and suspended as far as the top of the enclosing walls. Glass: two panes of 6 mm extra-clear float glass, 0.78 mm PVB interlayer, with frosted finish to underside. A total of 705 panes are used, each 1.45 x 1.45 m. Daylight penetrates the double-skin façade, enters the 2-m-deep cavity above the non-loadbearing enclosing walls and radiates evenly down through the glass ceiling. The frameless, individual bays of glass are left exposed; the 12-mm-wide joints are left open and are intended to lead the viewer to surmise the presence of the concealed, deep cavity and artificial lighting installation. A special trolley was designed for erection and maintenance of the glass ceilings. The automated lifting and moving of the glass to its allotted place not only simplified the job of erection but also meant that the frosted, exposed surface was protected against becoming too dirty through frequent handling.

A total of 666 specially developed pendant light fittings, each with a 58 W fluorescent tube and diffusor, were installed above the glass ceilings. They are controlled by the "Luxamate Professional" lighting management system which has several programs available. A so-called "Daylight Program" constantly adapts the artificial lighting to the ambient conditions. Spotlights and floodlights for special effects supplement the general amenity lighting.

Internal climate and energy concept

The underlying principle of the air-conditioning system employed here is based on two physical principles: firstly, the active coupling of internal climate and building mass, and secondly, the definition of a twin-zone model. The mass coupling takes into account the fact that periodic and aperiodic disturbances due to heat sources (visitors, daylight, artificial lighting) are to a large extent stored by temperature-controlled walls, floors and ceilings. Consequently, the air-conditioning plant functions with much lower flow rates (500 m^3/h instead of 12,500 m^3/h per storey). The twin-zone model separates the more disturbing, dry thermal loads of the daylight and artificial lighting in the space above the glass ceilings from the less disturbing thermal loads caused by visitors. While in modern, air-conditioned art galleries an air-change rate of four to eight times per hour is common, the Bregenz gallery manages with a figure of just 0.2.

A special feature of the concept is the consequential ground coupling. A dense network of water-filled plastic pipes is embedded in the 25-m-deep diaphragm walls which are surrounded by groundwater currents. This network of pipes within the diaphragm walls, and all walls and floor slabs, enables the mass of the building to be be cooled with the cooling capacity of the subsoil alone. Hence, the Bregenz gallery may well be the first air-conditioned art gallery without a refrigerating plant and dominating air ducts.

Site plan, scale 1:5000.

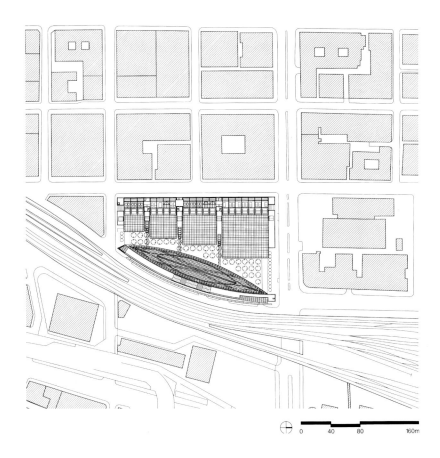

0 40 80 160m

Section through atrium,
scale 1:750.

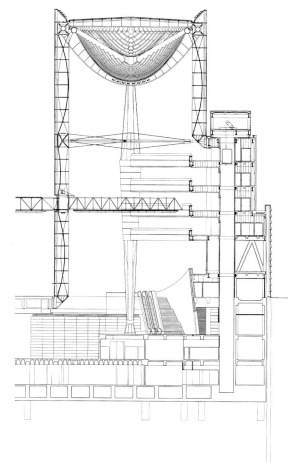

The great convex construction of the atrium follows the curve of the railway. The four square hall structures are arranged along the connecting plaza.

International Forum, Tokyo
Rafael Viñoly

In November 1989 an international jury, which included I.M. Pei, Fumihiko Maki, Kenzo Tange, Vittorio Gregotti and Arthur Erickson, had the task of picking the winner from among 350 designs for the Tokyo International Forum submitted by architects from 50 countries. Rafael Viñoly was awarded first prize and the contract. It was the first international competition of its kind ever to be held in Japan. The forum was to be located between the outer gardens of the Emperor's Palace and Tokyo's famous shopping and entertainment district, Ginza, on the site of the former city hall, built in 1957 to a design by Kenzo Tange. This building had been demolished in 1990 following the construction of the new city hall in the form of twin towers – again by Kenzo Tange – to the west in the Shinju-ku district of the city.

The site is bounded to the east by the railway lines of JR Yaman and the tracks of the *Shinkansen* high-speed train. To the west the boundary is marked by Metropolitan Road 402. Four underground railway lines and the extremely busy Tokyo und Yarakucho stations lie to the north and south. These ensure a very high influx of pedestrians to this area.

The Tokyo International Forum is Japan's largest public building, built in just five years at a total cost of over US-$ 1.2 billion. The internal layout serves both cultural and commercial functions and aims to instigate synergies between art and the economy.

A public concourse runs through the complex in a north-south direction and leads to a landscaped plaza. To the west of this axis are the four events halls: a 5,000-seat theatre, a multipurpose hall for up to 3,000 people, a concert hall with

Location
Tokyo International Forum, Metropolitan Road 402, Tokyo, Japan

Client
Tokyo Metropolitan Government, 2-8-1 Nishi-Shinjuku, Tokyo, Japan 163-01

Architects
Rafael Viñoly Architects, New York, NY with Masao Shina Architects, GKK Architects and Engineers

Structural engineers
Structural Design Group, Umezawa Structural Engineers, Hanawa Structural Engineers, Sasaki Structural Consultants, Yokoyama Structural Engineers

Lighting design
Claude R. Engle, Lighting Consultant, Lighting Planners Associates

Date of completion
1996

Plan, ground floor,
scale 1:2000.

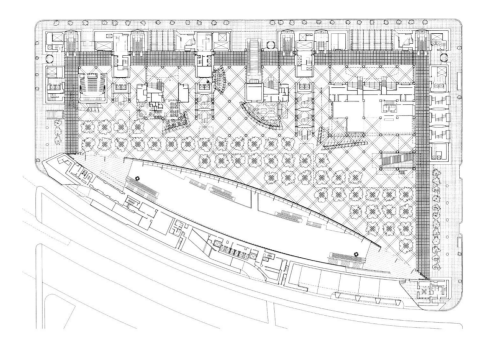

Plan, 1st basement level,
scale 1:2000.

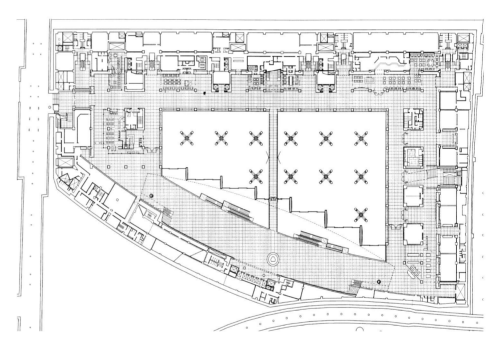

seating for 1,500 and an experimental theatre for an audience of 600. Beneath the
plaza there is an exhibition area of 18,250 m². The foyer serving all four halls is in
the form of a great glass atrium which in the east, alongside the railway lines, encompasses the conference centre.

The glass atrium

This striking construction is 207 m long, 32 m wide in the middle and 60 m high,
and is dominated by the 210-m-long supporting steel structure weighing 3,000 t; it
is supported on just two columns at a height of 52 m and both ends cantilever
some 40 m! The steel ribs of the roof structure, each pair of which is different,
connect two independent supporting structures for the flat glass roof: the compression ring around the edge of the roof and the compression arches joined to the
tops of the columns. The two columns gain lateral support by being connected to
the 4th and 7th floors of the conference centre, where they are 4.5 m in diameter;
at the ends these twin-walled steel columns are 1.3 m in diameter. They are filled
with concrete for stability.

The steelwork for the ship's hull-type supporting structure employed a specially hardened steel developed in Japan. This material can withstand temperatures of up to 600°C without any loss of loadbearing capacity. Therefore, separate fire protection was not necessary, a coat of paint sufficed. Assembled and welded, the steelwork was initially placed on temporary works at a height of 60 m before being lowered onto the columns. In his notes referring to the conception of the building, Rafael Viñoly describes how the atrium came about:

"The evolution of the design is the result of an unusually productive collaboration with Kunio Watanabe who, like most Japanese structural engineers, also has the mind of an architect. The outcome of this cooperation shows how we can benefit from bridging the occupational barriers which exist between architects, engineers and contractors. The structure of the building stems from the careful consideration of the path of the main loads and forces down to the foundations and the controlled formation of these paths. The amendments to the original design for the roof are perhaps the most significant developments to take place after winning the competition. These were the result of rethinking the relationship between the wall construction and the columns supporting the roof. Originally, huge triangular columns were planned along the curve of the glass wall which connected the vertical columns for the roof with a rigid framework in order to absorb the wind forces on this vast expanse of wall. After a lengthy analysis of the correlations between these forces and the span of the roof, a number of alternative systems were put forward. These investigations began with a step-by-step reduction in the number and dimensions of the columns along the glass wall and ended with the elimination of

Glass bridges made from laminated safety glass link the four halls with the atrium via the open plaza.

119

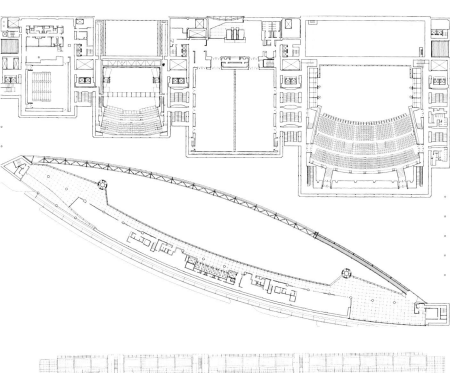

Plan, 5th floor, scale 1:2000.

Longitudinal section through hall structures, scale 1:2000.

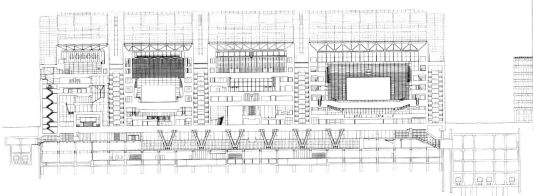

Longitudinal section through
the glass roof over the
entrance to the plaza.

Two completely independent
constructions form the
supporting structure for the
glass roof of the 207 m
long, max. 32 m wide and
60 m high atrium: the
compression ring around the
edge of the roof and the
compression arches joined to
the two columns, which
carry the ship's hull-type
supporting steelwork. On
the left, the vast glass wall
of the internal plaza; on the
right, alongside the railway
tracks, the conference centre.

Detail of trussed glass wall.
The glazing units were
supplied in frames and
installed on site.

The glass roof over the
southern entrance from the
Yurakucho underground to
the plaza is supported by
glass beams made from
laminated safety glass.

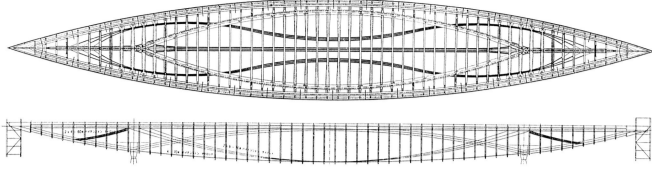

Plan and longitudinal section of atrium roof steelwork, scale 1:750.

the columns on the side of the building altogether. The side columns were replaced by two main internal columns, whereby the transfer of the forces was changed from the short span to the long span. The original building envelope, dominated by the transverse roof girders spanning onto the side columns, was transformed by a 200-m-long girder spanning the entire length of the glass atrium. The design of this roof was the subject of intensive study and philosophical debate. The concept of the roof as a transparent lattice originally provided for triangular areas. The intention of utilizing the double curve was based on a number of solutions which all centred on harmonizing the visual impression of the roof with its structural behaviour. Finally, we hit upon the idea of juxtaposing the three bending moment diagrams for the roof structure, the outcome of sketches produced at the same time as the design of the models for the diagrams. The structural loads are clearly expressed in the architecture of the roof. Cables follow the lines of tension on the surface of the volume, while two parabolic arcs discharge the compression (and the rainwater) into the columns. These two systems are connected with each other via a series of ribs which are sized in proportion to the loads and accommodate the shear forces."

The shallow pitched glass roof above the supporting structure is comprised of insulating glass.

The 600–m–long and 9–m–wide glass floor (laminated safety glass with a white, translucent interlayer) on the plaza above the exhibition area. It allows daylight to penetrate through to the lower levels. The surface of the laminated safety glass on the floor has been given a grid–type, non–slip finish by means of sand–blasting.

The glass walls of the atrium

As the roof structure is carried by just two monumental internal columns, the glass walls were able to be suspended as independent constructions from the roof. The tendency of the roof, supported at just two points, to tip about its longitudinal axis is counteracted by the supporting structure for the glass walls placed at 10.5 m centres. The trussed sag rods for the glazing bars are prestressed and transfer the horizontal forces acting on the 60-m-high glass wall of the plaza into two horizontal girders. The upper longitudinal girder is connected to the conference wing by means of two trussed transverse girders. The lower girder is formed by a ramp which links the audience levels of the theatre with the levels of the conference centre. It is linked to the conference centre via connecting bridges. The ramp leads to a glazed public gallery in the conference centre which provides a view of the Ginza district and Tokyo Bay. Above, the glass wall projects beyond the roof. Rooflight vents ensure a natural change of air and also serve as smoke vents. The glass walls, like the rest of the building, are designed to withstand earthquakes. Earthquake loadings are absorbed by allowing the 2.6 m x 2.5 m laminated safety glass panes made from heat-treated glass to slide across each other within the column-and-beam construction.

Longitudinal section and
plan, entrance floor.

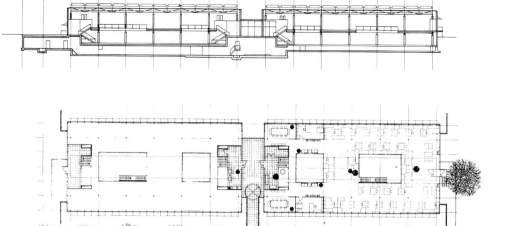

Isometric view.

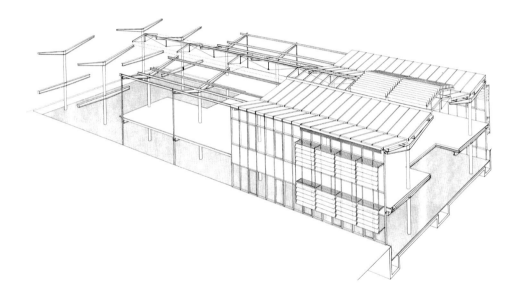

The aluminium louvres above
the flat rooflight are arranged parallel so that in the
vertical position they do not
obstruct the smoke vents.
They are 480 mm wide and
spaced at 380 mm centres.

Trussed rooflight construction. The rooflight at the
ridge has a width of 2 x
2.55 m.

Design office, Gartner & Co., Gundelfingen
Kurt Ackermann + Partner

The idea behind this office building was to create optimum working conditions for the 120 engineers and technicians at the location of this company, best known for its façade designs. As the architect, Kurt Ackermann, writes: "All working positions were designed to have an identical ambient quality so that hierarchical structures would not arise in the first place. The quality of the light at each workplace played a crucial role. Lighting conditions for every member of staff were to be optimized, both for drawing board and computer screen. The architectural result is a pilot run, like in car manufacture; further developments are to be worked out." Apart from that, the client's wish to express the company's own technology in an appropriate manner in the building had a considerable influence on the design. This was accomplished in a convincing and unpretentious manner by choosing the most modest solution for each component in relation to expenditure and efficiency. The intention was to demonstrate that quality architecture and innovative technology can be achieved at a reasonable price.

The shape and structure of the two-storey building are based on the notion of optimum use of daylight. The following functions had to be fulfilled in this respect: an effective rooflight at the ridge to illuminate the middle of this 20-m-deep building, reflecting and directing daylight into the interior, sunshading and glare protection for roofs and façades as well as the inclusion of the "integral façade" developed by Gartner. This façade fulfils two functions: support as well as heating or cooling. The steel structure consists of a frame of hollow sections joined to form a pipeline system through which hot water flows. This heating system encompasses the entire external wall and renders additional radiators superfluous. The integral façade can also be used for cooling in summer.

A pair of two-storey pavilions, each 42 x 21 m, is linked by a central entrance foyer. Each pavilion has 75 workplaces spread over two floors. The underlying structural concept involves a freestanding "table" for the intermediate floor and a "floating" roof construction above. The main loadbearing members are Y-shaped steel frames at 6.8 m centres which extend over both floors and comprise hollow-section columns with steel beams and cantilevers. The span between the columns is 13.6 m and the cantilever arms span 3.4 m to the sides, 4.2 m to the middle. Floor

Location
Josef Gartner & Co.,
89421 Gundelfingen,
Germany

Client
Josef Gartner & Co.

Architects
Prof. Dr techn. h.c. Kurt Ackermann with Jürgen Feit, Munich

Assistance
Marianne Habermann, Bettina Hamann

Structural engineers
Dr.-Ing. Bernhard Behringer, Walter Müller, Munich

Building services
Ing.-Büro Dr Karl Pitscheider, Munich

Thermal & acoustic consultants
Prof. Dr.-Ing. habil. Karl Gertis, Prof. Dr.-Ing. Walter E. Fuchs, Stuttgart

Glazing
Josef Gartner & Co.

Date of completion
1993

Section.

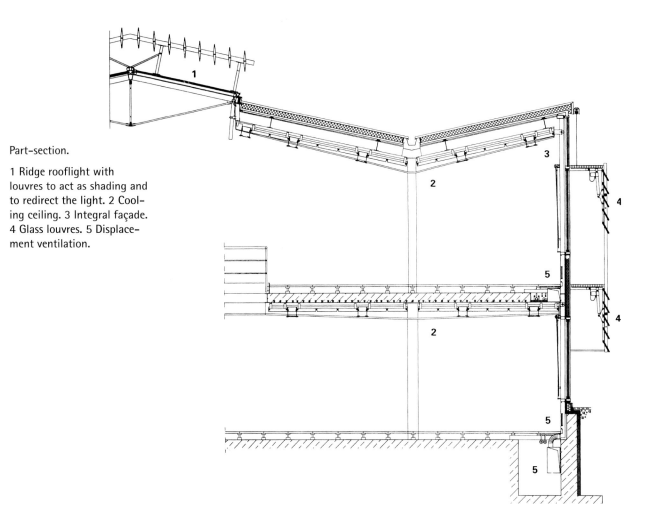

Part-section.

1 Ridge rooflight with
louvres to act as shading and
to redirect the light. 2 Cooling ceiling. 3 Integral façade.
4 Glass louvres. 5 Displace-
ment ventilation.

beams and cantilever roof beams are tied to façade posts. The intermediate floor is a composite floor slab with two openings, one 6.8 x 11.80 m and the other 6.8 x 6.8 m, in each pavilion so that light from the rooflight can penetrate through to the lower floor level.

Façade construction

The integral façade is glazed with 3-ply insulating glass having two low-emissivity coatings and argon gas in the cavity, U value 0.9 W/m²K. The thermal separation between heated supporting structure and external skin results in virtually no additional heat loss. The physicist C. Scholz explains this phenomenon: "The energy consumption of an integral façade is determined by two factors. Firstly, reaching the temperature necessary for a comfortable internal climate, and secondly, the quality of the thermal separation to the outside. The temperature experienced by humans is different to the actual air temperature. It can be approximated to the average of the internal air temperature and the ambient surface temperature. This means that a higher ambient surface temperature permits a lower internal air temperature without this drop in air temperature being noticed by the occupants. Let us take the example of an unheated external wall with an ambient surface temperature of 17°C. In this case the internal air temperature must be heated up to 23°C in order to achieve a perceived temperature of 20°C. If the façade is heated to give an ambient surface temperature of 20°C, then the internal air temperature need only be 20°C as well. So in this example, the internal air temperature with a heated façade can be set 3°C lower than would be necessary with an unheated façade. Compared with conventional heating systems, using radiators for instance, this achieves a marked saving in energy."

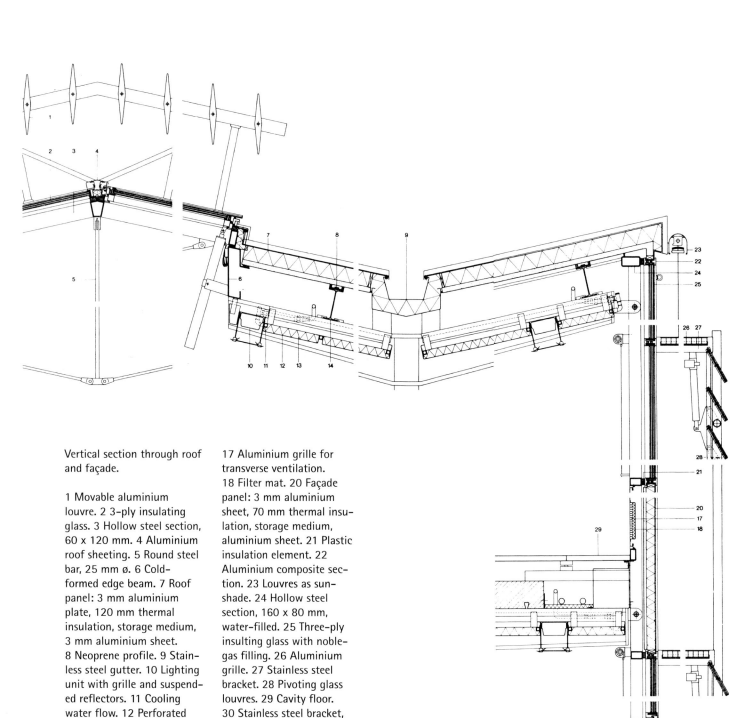

Vertical section through roof and façade.

1 Movable aluminium louvre. 2 3-ply insulating glass. 3 Hollow steel section, 60 x 120 mm. 4 Aluminium roof sheeting. 5 Round steel bar, 25 mm ø. 6 Cold-formed edge beam. 7 Roof panel: 3 mm aluminium plate, 120 mm thermal insulation, storage medium, 3 mm aluminium sheet. 8 Neoprene profile. 9 Stainless steel gutter. 10 Lighting unit with grille and suspended reflectors. 11 Cooling water flow. 12 Perforated aluminium sheet as cooling surface. 13 Acoustic insulation. 14 Steel beam, IPE 240.

17 Aluminium grille for transverse ventilation. 18 Filter mat. 20 Façade panel: 3 mm aluminium sheet, 70 mm thermal insulation, storage medium, aluminium sheet. 21 Plastic insulation element. 22 Aluminium composite section. 23 Louvres as sunshade. 24 Hollow steel section, 160 x 80 mm, water-filled. 25 Three-ply insulting glass with noble-gas filling. 26 Aluminium grille. 27 Stainless steel bracket. 28 Pivoting glass louvres. 29 Cavity floor. 30 Stainless steel bracket, 1.5 mm thick. 31 Bituminous waterproofing.

Escape and maintenance balconies projecting from the north and south sides at the same time serve as supports for glass louvres which provide shade and also redirect the incoming light. The shading of both floors consists of frameless, hinged glass louvres made from toughened safety glass, 10 mm thick, 300 mm wide. These louvres are placed 900 mm in front of the façade as a second layer and are combined to form units extending over two bays (2 x 6.8 m). The louvres are connected via their centre axis to the central control system and the glass is provided with a weatherproof reflective coating.

When the sky is completely overcast or the sun is at a very high altitude or no sunlight shines directly onto the façade, then the louvres can be pivoted to allow the maximum view through to the outside from the inside. This position of the louvres allows daylight to be directed by the reflective coating onto the diffusely reflective ceiling, thus brightening the lower levels of the building. Improvements in lighting intensity can be achieved in room depths of 4.5-6.5 m by using glass louvres to redirect the light, the optimum depth being about 5.3 m. A value of 430 lux is attained without glass louvres and 1000 lux with them. In addition, glass louvres also have the advantage that when closed or nearly closed, vision is not impaired.

As neighbouring buildings forced the level of the basement to be about 1.90 m below ground, an embankment has been provided in front of the façade which begins at window-sill level and slopes up at 30°. To improve the low level of daylight in the basement, the original plan had been to fit a strip of reflectors along the embankment in order to direct daylight into the room or onto the underside of the cooled ceiling. Simulation calculations were performed in order to establish the most effective degree of such reflection. Normal soil with 20% reflectance, light-coloured gravel with 60% reflectance and metal reflectors with 80% reflectance and 50% specular reflection were simulated and compared. Compared with the gravel, the reflectors improved the lighting intensity at a distance of 5 m by just 7%. This was uneconomic, considering the high cost of the reflectors compared to the gravel. Apart from that, the reflectors could have only been set up on the north side as on the south side for most of the time they would have reflected undesirable rays of sunlight into the interior and thus heated up the room.

Antiglare blinds made of a fibreglass fabric are fitted to the inside of the façades. Their light transmission of 10% permits a practically unobstructed view of the outside world. The antiglare blinds can be operated individually and allow those working with computers in particular to determine the optimum level of illumination and glare penetrating the glass louvres.

Ridge rooflight

A glass roof with a width of 2 x 2.55 m and a pitch of 12° was included along the entire length of the building in order to improve the internal illumination in the middle. Fitted above the glass is sunshading comprising pivoting, plain aluminium louvres made from from anodized, extruded sections. When the sun is at a low altitude, the louvres are vertical; when the sun is high in the sky, they are tilted slightly to the north. Similar to a northlight roof, this allows diffuse light to enter the building but excludes direct sunlight. The transparency of the system was optimized by a slim louvre profile (60 mm at the axis of rotation) and a light-coloured, diffusely reflective surface. The large lightwells in the floor enable the overhead illumination gained via the rooflight to reach the lower level and thus make a major contribution to increasing the use of daylight in the basement. The reflective, cooling ceiling ensures that the light is evenly distributed over the depth of the room. This ceiling consists of white, powder-coated aluminium sheets with water-filled sections. The cooling and heating effects are achieved by solar radiation. Therefore, the unpleasant draughts associated with dynamic cooling systems are avoided with this system.

Building management system

All components for an optimum internal climate – heating, cooling, ventilation, heat recovery, sunshading, lighting and fire protection – are controlled and regulated by the "Direct Digital Control" (DDC) management system. The sensors and servomotors are connected to the master computer via five intelligent substations by means of a bus, i.e. a wiring system for control impulses. This wiring system is separate from the actual power supply to the devices and, like a bus route, supplies the control impulses for the devices, for example, the glass sunshading louvres, arranged like "bus stops" along the route. To do this, the computer analyses all relevant data such as angle of incident radiation and whether sunlight is actually striking the glass surfaces at all. The computer then makes adjustments, for example, to the angle of the louvres, depending on the outcome of its analysis. In order to avoid continuous movement of the sunshading in the case of rapidly changing skies, average values for the radiation intensity are used as signals for the drives.

Pivoting glass louvres made from toughened safety glass, 10 mm thick, 300 mm wide, as a second skin 900 mm in front of the façade.

The view across the building shows the high daylight ratio inside.

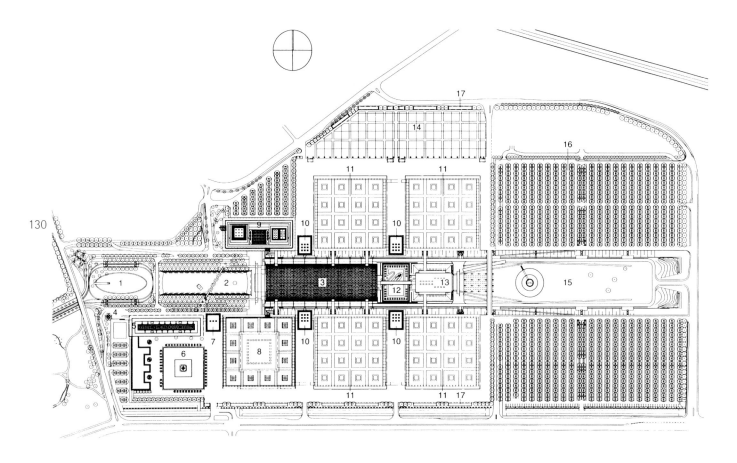

130

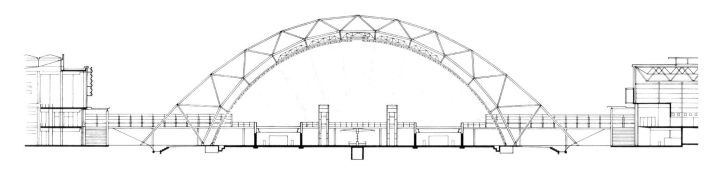

Site plan, scale 1:8000.

1 Forecourt. 2 Reservoir.
3 West Entrance Hall.
4 Tower. 5 Offices. 6 Workshops. 7 Forum. 8 Taller
exhibition hall. 9 Conference
zone. 10 Restaurant.
11 Standard exhibition hall.
12 Park. 13 East Entrance
Hall. 14 Open-air exhibition
space. 15 East Park. 16 Car
park. 17 Services.

Section through West En-
trance Hall, scale 1:1000.

Detail of cast arm frog's
fingers.

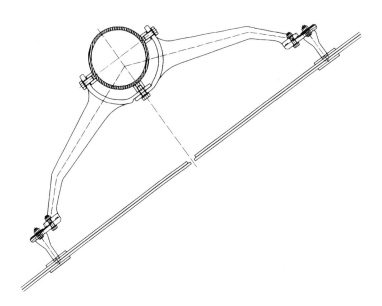

Glass halls for the Leipzig Exhibition Grounds
Volkwin Marg

Situated at the crossroads of important European trading routes, Leipzig had already become an important market-place by the 12th century. After Emperor Maximilian I granted the city the right to hold trade fairs in 1497, the significance of Leipzig as a venue for exhibitions and fairs steadily grew until the changes brought about by the unification of Germany in October 1990 demanded a new structure for the grounds. During the period of the German Democratic Republic, Leipzig had been the main showcase for the state economies of the Eastern Bloc. However, this function became obsolete and, in addition, Leipzig now had to contend with national and international competition. In the light of this situation, the City Council took the decision in October 1991 – with a three-quarters majority – not to refurbish the existing inner-city exhibition grounds but instead to relocate them north of the city on the site of the former Leipzig-Mockau trade-fair aerodrome, 7 km from the main railway station, with good links to the motorway network and not far from Halle-Leipzig Airport at Schkeuditz.

Fifteen architects from Denmark, Germany, England and the Netherlands were invited in November 1991 to take part in a two-round competition. In April 1992 the architects from the Aachen office of Gerkan, Marg und Partner were awarded 1st prize. To Jan Esche's question asking what he considered to be the qualities of his design, Volkwin Marg replied: "There are many aspects and I'll limit myself to just two for now. The fascinating design from the Richard Rogers Partnership (3rd prize) had the desired operational density but lacked an urban or rural interaction with its surroundings. It represented a brilliant engineering solution in a somewhat indifferent, insular position. By contrast, the animating, poetical design from Sudau, Storch & Ehlers (2nd prize) extolled the vision of a spacious park landscape with visitors strolling leisurely among loosely arranged exhibitions. However, the distances for visitors and exhibitors were too great. Our design united the advantages of both – the spacious park with the compact trade fair."

As the site for the new Leipzig trade fair possessed absolutely no rural qualities amid the amorphous settlements on the northern edge of the city, the architects transformed the 2-km-long, trapezoidal site by way of a trench, 150 m wide and 5 m deep. At its western end, the trench accommodates the railway station

Location
Neue Messe Leipzig,
Messeallee 1,
04356 Leipzig, Germany

Client
Leipziger Messeges. mbH

Architects
gmp - von Gerkan, Marg und
Partner, Aachen and Leipzig

Design
Volkwin Marg

Project Manager
Hubert Nienhoff

Steel & glass central hall
gmp, Leipzig, with Ian Ritchie
Architects, London

Structural engineers
Ing.-Büro Polonyi & Partner,
Cologne, with Ing.-Büro
H.Haringer, Munich

Steel-and-glass construction
(central hall)
Mero-Raumstruktur GmbH,
Würzburg, Seele GmbH,
Gersthofen

Office building
Seele GmbH, Gersthofen, and
Fries, Obersulm

Printed glass
BGT Bischoff Glastechnik
GmbH, Bretten

Date of completion
1996

Gable on east side with
access via glazed footbridge
from eastern entrance.

"Messebahnhof", i.e. local public transport, and in the east, road transport, with parking space for 6,000 visitors' and 1,000 exhibitors' vehicles. In the centre stands the glass barrel-vault construction of the West Entrance Hall, 244 m long, 80 m wide and 30 m high. It is reminiscent of that great tradition of glass architecture, namely the classic roofs of the great 19th century railway stations, but applying the resources of the 20th. This access concourse is flanked by two 8-m-high standard halls on each side, each offering 20,500 m^2 of exhibition space. Another 20,500 m^2 of space is available in a higher hall on the southern side, with 12-16 m clear head-room. This higher hall is supported on just four columns, leaving a clear area of 75 x 75 m inside. Each of the standard halls has nine columns and can offer uninter-rupted floor areas measuring 37.5 x 37.5 m. All halls have vehicular access on three sides.

West Entrance Hall

The great glass-and-steel structure forming the central hall represents not only a landmark of international calibre for Leipzig's new exhibition grounds but also for the city itself. The architects did not want a reflective outer skin and so opted for an exposed, external supporting structure from which the glazing is suspended. The barrel vault is a perfect circular segment with a primary supporting structure com-posed of a curved square grid of welded steel tubes. The shell is stiffened every 25 m by arched space-frame trusses, also made from steel tubes, to withstand snow and wind loads. The gables at the eastern and western ends are self-support-ing, separate structures comprising concentric "ladders", one above the other, with fixed bases. They are interlocked radially with each other by means of a Vierendeel arch with a torsion-resistant base. A special construction enables the use of elec-tromagnetically secured escape doors; in an emergency, they slide upwards at an angle and so leave an unimpeded escape route.

Plan of ground floor
West Entrance Hall.

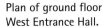

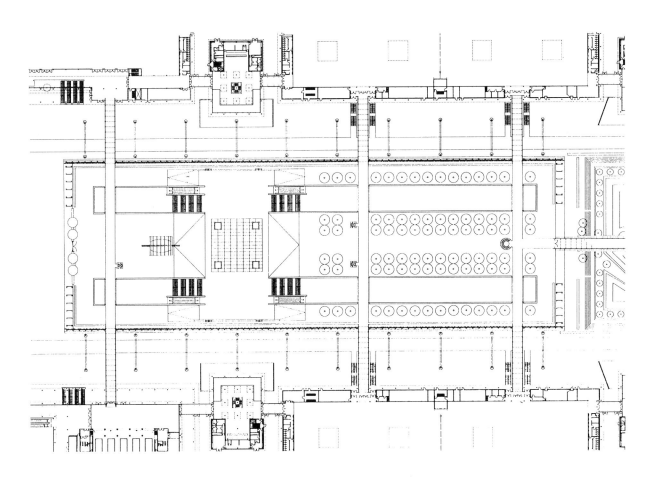

Glazing to the barrel-vault roof

The great hall, 244 x 80 m, 30 m to the crown and 35 m high overall, is covered with 26,050 m^2 of glass, 5687 m^2 of this printed with a striped pattern of ceramic inks to provide solar-control and antiglare properties. The laminated safety glass, consisting of two single panes of safety glass each 10 mm thick, are made from extra-clear, i.e. low iron oxide, float glass. All panes are a standard 3105 x 1524 mm. The fixings for the panes were developed in conjunction with Ian Ritchie. Stainless steel fixings with a floating mount, which can be slid along the X and Y axes to secure the glass free from secondary bending moments, are screwed to arms, so-called frog's fingers, of GGG 40 spheroidal graphite cast iron. Every pane is held at four points. Joints are sealed with silicone. A total of 9,800 cast arms and 22,500 fixings were installed.

Glass assembly

As work below the glass roof was proceeding at the same time, the glass could not be installed using conventional scaffolding. Therefore, Seele GmbH, responsible for erecting the glazing, devised a new method. The panes of glass were fitted by working down from the crown. An electrically driven trolley moved on rails over the outer radius of the barrel vault and transported every pane of glass exactly to its allotted position. The panes, with fixings already in place, were clipped into the trolley. At the appropriate position, the mechanical fixings were secured and the pane of glass unclipped from the trolley. Thanks to this method, the glass could be erected during the winter and erection of the 5,526 panes completed within seven months.

The glass envelope is suspended inside the structure and reflects activities in the hall.

View through central hall.

Trussed glass roof construction to office building.

Building Inspectorate approvals

In accordance with German construction law, special approval was required prior to construction of this glass structure with its individual bolted fixings. This involved proving that the overhead glazing had adequate residual strength after breakage to prevent the immediate failure of a pane of the laminated safety glass used here. The panes held by means of individual bolted fixings were tested under a uniformly distributed load, the impact loads of soft and hard bodies, and a long-term static load. The tests were performed on undamaged as well as damaged panes of laminated safety glass in which either the upper or the lower single pane of safety glass was ruined. Darmstadt Technical University and Seele GmbH ran a total of 47 test series.

Erecting the glass.

Air-conditioning and heating

A build-up of heat and solar radiation below the great glass roof is primarily prevented by natural convention currents. Opening glass louvres, located at the base of each side, allow fresh air from outside to enter the building. The warm air can escape upwards via vents in the centre, along the crown. The smooth, frameless glazing offers particularly streamlined surfaces for the thermal currents. In addition, the external supporting structure shades about 15% of the surface subjected to solar radiation and the panes printed with a striped pattern prevent overheating in critical areas. Furthermore, an external washing system using decalcified water can be set up in such a way that with a thin distribution, a natural evaporative cooling effect is achieved. In summer cold water can be pumped through the underfloor heating system to create a cooling effect. In winter the 20,000 m^2 of stone flooring is heated. At the same time, this area is a mass storage medium for the incident solar radiation. When the hall is not in use, this storage medium keeps the building free from frost. When in use it balances out the day-night fluctuations.

Vents at the crown of the glass barrel-vault roof over the entrance hall.

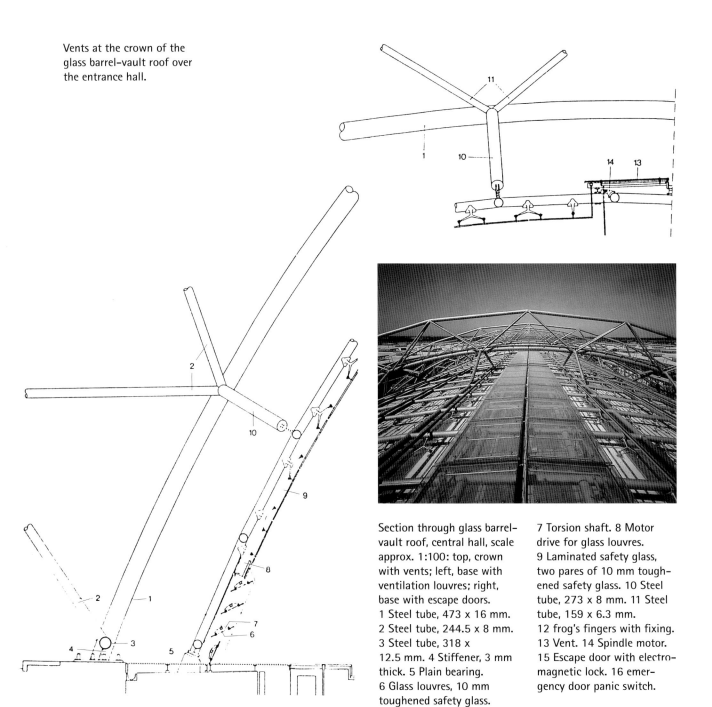

Section through glass barrel-vault roof, central hall, scale approx. 1:100: top, crown with vents; left, base with ventilation louvres; right, base with escape doors.
1 Steel tube, 473 x 16 mm.
2 Steel tube, 244.5 x 8 mm.
3 Steel tube, 318 x 12.5 mm. 4 Stiffener, 3 mm thick. 5 Plain bearing.
6 Glass louvres, 10 mm toughened safety glass.
7 Torsion shaft. 8 Motor drive for glass louvres.
9 Laminated safety glass, two pares of 10 mm toughened safety glass. 10 Steel tube, 273 x 8 mm. 11 Steel tube, 159 x 6.3 mm.
12 frog's fingers with fixing.
13 Vent. 14 Spindle motor.
15 Escape door with electro-magnetic lock. 16 emergency door panic switch.

Glazed footbridges

The exhibition halls are linked to the upper level of the glass hall by means of glazed footbridges. The 12 mm curved toughened safety glass used is held in place by individual bolted fixings. The panes are 1650 mm long in the curved direction and 3250 mm in the other. All panes had to undergo a heat-soak test. This involves heating them after toughening in order to test them for the occurrence of nickel sulphide inclusions, which expand upon changes of temperature and can lead to breakage of the glass.

About one-fifth of the glass is printed with a solar-control pattern.

Glass roof to office block

The office building serving the trade fair grounds, at the western entrance, includes a large atrium, 120 x 12.5 m, with a glass roof. In this case the supporting structure is on the inside and the frameless glass skin on the outside. The curved steel tubes, ø 88.9 mm with 7.1 mm walls, are trussed with a delicate, cable lattice. The laminated safety glass comprising 6 and 8 mm thick float glass panes are fastened by means of individual bolted fixings attached to cast X-pieces sitting on saddles on the curved steel tubes.

135

Supporting structure on the outside. Glazed footbridge to exhibition hall.

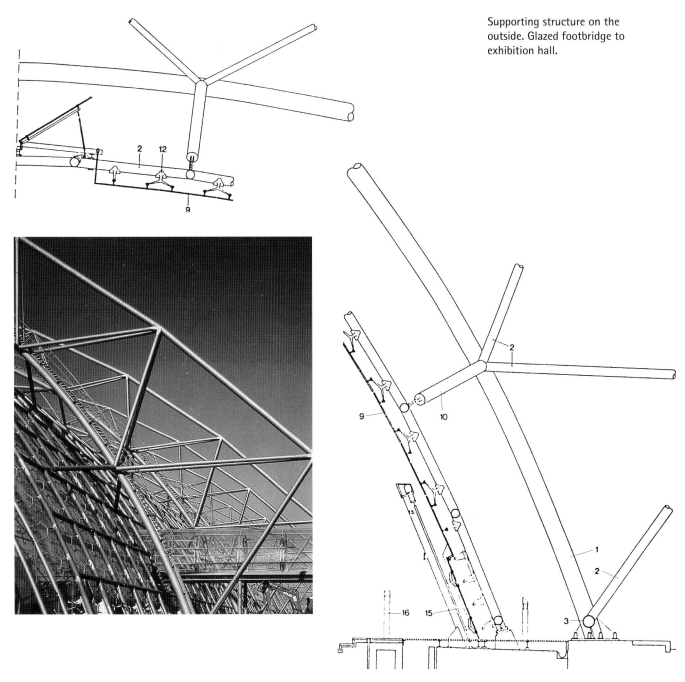

Plan of ground floor, *das Grosse Spiel*.

1 Forecourt. 2 Entrance hall. 3 Cloakroom. 4 Restaurant. 5 Inner courtyard. 6 Canteen. 7 Passageway.

Plan of basement, *das Grosse Spiel*.

1 Roulette hall. 2 Black Jack. 3 Baccara. 4 Cash desks. 5 Bistro. 6 Reception. 7 Toilets. 8 Existing basement garage.

Longitudinal section and plan, ground floor, slot machines area.

1 Entrance. 2 Cash desk. 3 Cloakroom. 4 Bar. 5 Toilets. 6 Slot machines.

Section and plan of glass staircase.

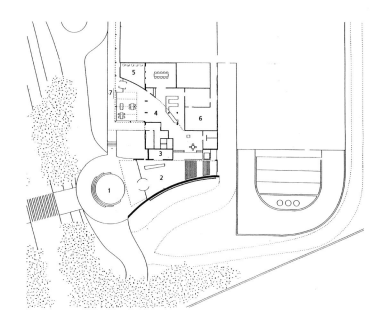

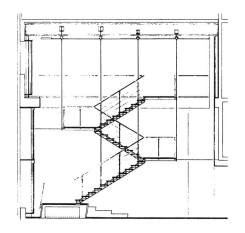

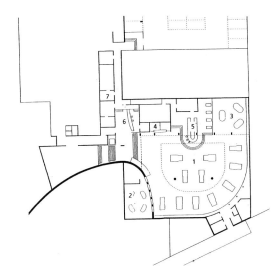

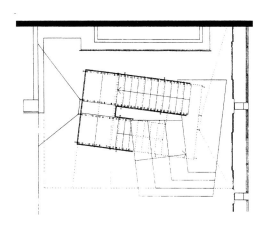

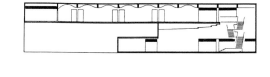

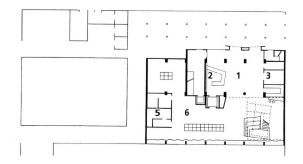

Trussed canopy of laminated safety glass over main entrance. The hoar-frost in this photo makes the transparent glass roof appear opaque.

The minimal structure results in an extraordinarily transparent entrance façade.

Stuttgart Casino
Manfred Aichele and Wolfgang Fiedler

The amendment to the Gambling Establishments Act by the State Government of Baden-Württemberg in February 1995 meant that besides Baden-Baden and Constance, Stuttgart was now able to become the third city with a casino in that federal state. One criterion for the site was that it should have a direct link to a multistorey or underground car park. This requirement was satisfied by the "Stuttgart International" (SI) Leisure and Adventure Centre on the southern edge of the city, well served by all forms of transport. The layout allocated 1300 m^2 to slot machines and 2100 m^2 to *das Grosse Spiel* and a bistro. Both sections were accommodated by converting and extending the existing hotel complex within the SI Centre. Space was created in the area of the former indoor pool for the slot machines and in the area of the former bowling alley for *das Grosse Spiel*. Once the decision was made to locate the casino here, the design and construction timetable was extremely tight.

Slot machines area
Access to the slot machines area (*das Kleine Spiel*) is via the ground floor of the hotel tower. One disadvantage of the existing building was that the slot machines had to be housed on two levels; besides the ground floor, another space on the second floor had to be adapted as well. The low storey heights posed problems as well as a number of transverse shear walls – necessary for the stability of the high-rise block – which could not be altered. In addition, all the mechanical installations were suspended beneath the floor slabs. In order to create a more spacious entrance for the new casino, two floor bays were removed at second floor level. A staircase of glass and stainless steel was included to link the two levels and an illusion of more space was created by building the rear wall behind the stairs as a mirror extending over three storeys. This means that the second floor can be seen from the ground floor. A translucent glass wall placed in front of the existing window wall ensures an even distribution of daylight, which can be supplemented by artificial lighting.

Location
Spielbank Stuttgart,
Freizeit- und Erlebniszentrum
Stuttgart International,
Plieninger Strasse 100,
70567 Stuttgart-Möhringen,
Germany

Client
Stella Musical AG

Architects
Fiedler Aichele, BDA, Stuttgart

Assistance
Ariane Drögmöller, Harald
Krause, Michael Rauscher,
Sabine Weiss, Adelgunde
Wuppermann

Project Manager
Hajo Wehrmann, Stuttgart

Design of glass façade
Robert Danz, Schönaich

Construction of glass façade
MBM, Metallbau Möckmühl
GmbH, Möckmühl

Construction of artistic glass
wall in *das Grosse Spiel*
VEGLA-GVG Glasverarbeitung
Köln-Porz GmbH

Date of completion
1996

Plan of horizontal girder to the glass canopy over the entrance to *das Grosse Spiel*.

Plan of canopy glazing showing individual bolted fixings.

138

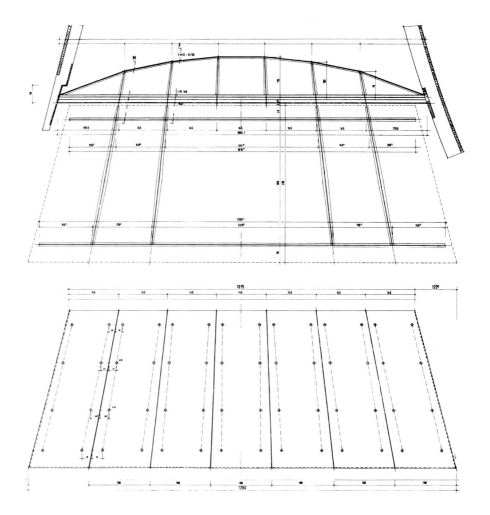

Glass stairs

The three flights, two intermediate landings and large base plinth of the staircase are made from 1.4301 stainless steel with a ground surface finish, 280 grit, and treads of laminated safety glass. The ground-floor plinth is formed by a concrete base on which a supporting structure of square hollow sections, 40 x 40 x 4 mm, is set up on a 500 x 500 mm grid, with resin anchors at every intersection. The treads, plinth and landing plate are clad in 1.4301 stainless steel sheet, 8 mm thick. These sheets are only hot-rolled, not exactly flat and with porous surfaces; therefore, they must be heated up in order to even them out prior to grinding and cutting by means of a water-jet technique. Only this method allows austenitic steel to be cut at an angle to its surface.

Along the edges, the cladding is welded on from underneath using the MAG arc-welding method. The joints in the tread and riser cladding are butt-welded and ground at an angle of 10°. To improve the sound insulation, all points of support are bedded on silicone in those areas not accessible for welding.

The stair flights are designed as lattice girders with tension/compression members, 20 mm diameter, and 50 x 8 mm flat bracing per tread unit. With a full landing load on one side, the loads in the tension/compression members are reversed; therefore, both members are of equal size. The hangers for the whole staircase are screwed into precisely located members with M20 internal threads attached to pre-assembled steelwork below the suspended ceiling. There are two hangers for each side of each stair flight. Here, the 50 x 8 mm flats below the treads are also connected to 50 x 5 mm flats. This is where the handrail uprights, two 50 x 6 mm flats, are welded on. The landing plates are set up for the glass plates at the same width as for the treads. Across the width of the stairwell between the flights, the landings

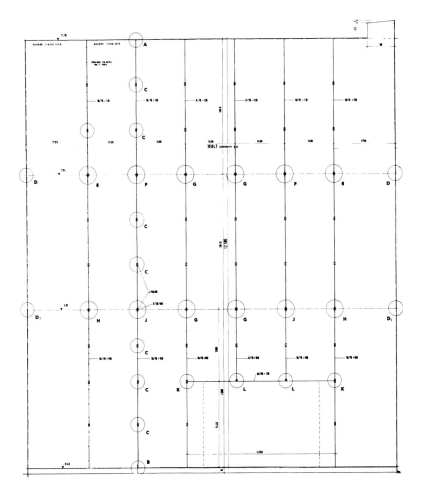

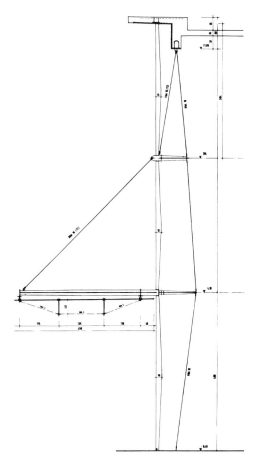

Elevation on glass curtain
wall at the entrance to *das
Grosse Spiel*.

Section through glass
curtain wall.

are rigidly welded over their full depth to a 10 mm plate. The surfaces of glass and sheet steel are flush at this point. This is the only point to which lateral bracing is attached –in the form of two pretensioned steel cables connected to both intermediate landings and positioned at an angle to the wall. The top landing is only welded on the exit side to the structure installed prior to laying the floor covering. The balustrading consists of twin uprights of 50 x 6 mm flats and a mesh of infill bars, ø 12 mm, and a handrail, ø 30 x 3 mm. The treads and the glazed landing plates comprise laminated safety glass, two 8 mm toughened glass panes and one 20 mm toughened glass pane, printed with a non-slip pattern. The glass is fastened and supported by means of individual bolted fixings.

Area for *das Grosse Spiel*

In the given circumstances, a fitting design for the room for *das Grosse Spiel* (roulette, black jack, baccara) could not be based on traditional examples and, according to the architects, should not express a false sense of security through a lack of conventional styling. Manfred Aichele described the design approach of the architects thus: "We thought that it must be possible to translate the gaiety of the Baroque into our present architectural language using contemporary artistic statements. In some instances we were able to utilize the materials of that period, for example, plaster, *stucco lustro* and mirrors; however, in other places we wanted to use new materials such as stainless steel, large expanses of glass and coloured glass surfaces." This approach led to glass becoming a distinctive design element in many details of the Stuttgart Casino.

Glass roof on individual
bolted fixings over the
bistro.

Translucent milk glass wall adjacent the glass staircase.

Glass staircase with stainless steel members in the hall for *das Kleine Spiel* in front of the storey-height mirror wall (left). Landings and treads are made from laminated

safety glass (2 x 8 mm toughened glass and 1 x 20 mm toughened glass, non-slip printing), stainless steel base plinth.

Wall of blue glassbricks, lit from behind.

The glass-and-steel entrance hall

The entrance façade of the area for *das Grosse Spiel* consists of two integrated structural components: the vertical façade of insulating glass and the projecting canopy of laminated safety glass. The stainless steel structure for the canopy, cantilevering some 4.5 m, penetrates the glass wall at the joints between the glass panes above the entrance. The horizontal forces due to canopy and wind loads on the façade are transferred to the concrete walls via two horizontal girders. The self-weight of the canopy, the girders and the glass above +4.5 m level is supported by patented Rodan ties fixed to the concrete beam at roof level.

Between the two girders, the tensile forces are taken by the stainless steel flats which extend into the joints between the panes. The stabilizing forces of the compression chords of the girders are transferred via slender Rodan ties into the floor slab and the concrete beam. The panes of insulating glass are supported at one-third and one-quarter points to resist the wind pressure; wind suction is catered for by a continuous fixing. Stainless steel flats extend into the joints between the panes to take the wind loads from the insulating glass. The inner panes of the insulating glass units, consisting of laminated safety glass and toughened safety glass, stabilize the compression chord of the flat section. The internal joints are left open, while the external, vertical joints are covered by cup-shaped, bent-up, stainless steel sections and the horizontal ones sealed with silicone and covered by thin stainless steel strips.

Glass canopy

The canopy structure over the entrance consists of a number of special stainless steel sections arranged above the glass itself. These are connected to the stainless steel girders behind the façade by means of struts and ties. All special sections were fabricated from flats and welded by laser. The trussed laminated safety glass of the canopy is split up into a fan arranagement and suspended below this steel structure.

Structural design

The calculations for steel and glass were carried out on separate structural systems with the aid of the ANSYS program suite. In designing the steel members of the entrance façade and canopy, the stiffening effect of the glass panes was not considered.

The calculations for the steel structure were perfomed by modelling the steelwork of the entrance façade and canopy structure by means of beam elements. The Rodan ties cannot be used for compressive loadings and so this was taken into account by means of non-linear calculation strategies. Checking the stability of the vertical stiffeners was carried out by means of detailed geometric, non-linear calculations on shell models.

To design the glass for the canopy, the stresses in the glass were determined by finite-element analyses on shell/solids models. In doing so, the holes for the glass fixings and the effect of the mountings in these was taken into consideration. Accurate modelling of these individual fixings was chosen in view of their mechanical action. Elastomeric layers and poured joints were incorporated. The trussing of the glass panes with Rodan ties was also included in the model.

Glass art

The 1995 art competition for the design of the glass wall in the roulette hall of *das Grosse Spiel* – 50 m long and 4 m high! – for invited participants was won by Hella Santarossa. Her design was inspired by the games themselves, with people coming and going across the entire area. The red and black, scored outlines of individuals, couples and groups play out scenes on an illuminated background varying from golden yellow to white to transparent. The work was produced on 49 panes of toughened safety glass, each 1.2 x 4.0 m and 10 mm thick, which are installed in the form of a horizontal rolling wall including emergency exits with swing doors. To produce the motifs, the pieces of glass were laid horizontally side by side in the same order in which they were to be finally installed vertically. The artist could then "float" over the glass surface to accomplish her designs. Ceramic inks were employed. Following the tempering process to form toughened safety glass, the surfaces of the 49 pieces were subjected to acid embossing and checked by a heat-soak test.

Section.

Plan of entrance level on the
rue du Saint-Esprit.

142

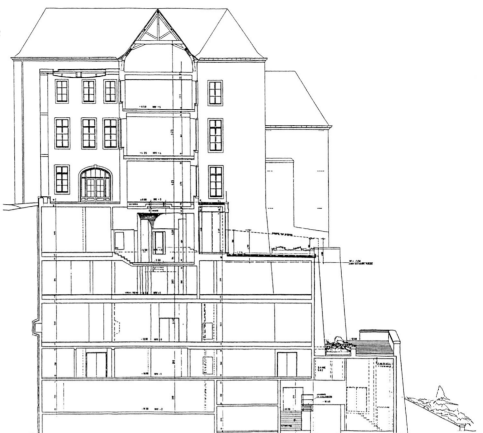

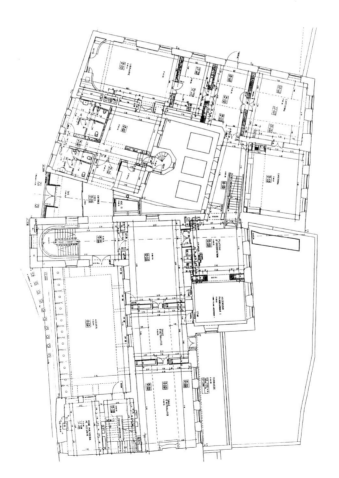

The roof appears to float owing to the glazing around the edge.

143

Luxembourg City History Museum
Conny Lentz and Repérages Architects

The opening of this museum for city history on 22 June 1996 marked the successful end to a creative process which had started way back in 1982 with a declaration of intent by the city council to establish just such a museum in order to reinforce "the public's response to its architectural heritage, [promote] further research into the city's history and [strengthen] the protection of public buildings". In the rue du Saint-Esprit, in the old part of the city, near to the Grand Duke's palace and the city hall, the council owned four houses which had previously belonged to aristocratic and merchant families, and had once formed part of the sanctuary of the Abbey of Orval. They housed the music conservatory, the offices of the education authority and the city's social services department. This group of buildings dated from the 17th, 18th and 19th centuries, and even showed traces from the Middle Ages; therefore, they had to be preserved.

After the music conservatory moved to new premises in Merl in 1985, the group of four historic buildings seemed an ideal location for the museum. The museum curator Danièle Wagener was taken on in 1986 and given the task of drawing up a concept for the museum and gathering together the various collections. Surveys of the buildings themselves began in 1987, followed by measures to strengthen the structure. A working party of historians, under the chairmanship of General Secretary Henri Beck, was set up to work out the museum programme. After this project was completed in 1992, work on the conversion of the buildings could begin.

As the surveys revealed, the existing space would not have been sufficient for the planned exhibitions. Therefore, it was decided to create extra space by digging into the bedrock. Some 20,000 m^3 of rock was excavated – enough for five floors below the level of the rue du Saint-Esprit. For the main entrance, the architect selected the former open area between house Nos. 14, 16 and 18 fronting the rue du Saint-Esprit. The original open area was re-created and given a full-height glass curtain wall. A second entrance at the lower level was provided at "Corniche".

The arrangement of the rooms by Repérages Architects combines old and new in a sensitive approach and creates a special, clear ambience in conjunction with light-coloured wood and old rubble masonry. The glazed panorama lift, with a floor area of 18 m^2 and a 27.7 m shaft, can take 65 passengers. This mammoth lift links

Location
Musée d'Histoire de la Ville de Luxembourg,
14 rue du Saint-Esprit,
2090 Luxembourg

Client
Luxembourg City Council

Architects
Conny Lentz, Luxembourg
Repérages Architects, Paris

Structural and services engineers
Gehl, Jacoby & Ass. s.a.r.l., Luxembourg

Glass construction
Magnus Müller GmbH,
35510 Butzbach, Germany

Planar system
Pilkington Flachglas AG,
Gelsenkirchen, Germany

Date of completion
1996

Glass elevation facing the rue du Saint-Esprit. On the left, the entrance; on the right, the reception area.

19 mm glass stiffeners stabilize the 12-m-high curtain wall made from toughened safety glass. The panes are connnected by means of stainless steel plates.

The exhibition rooms in the basement levels. Glass roof-lights have been incorporated in the vaulted ceilings dating from the Middle Ages.

The glass bonds old and new.

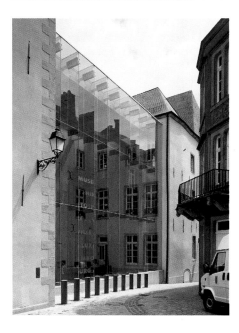

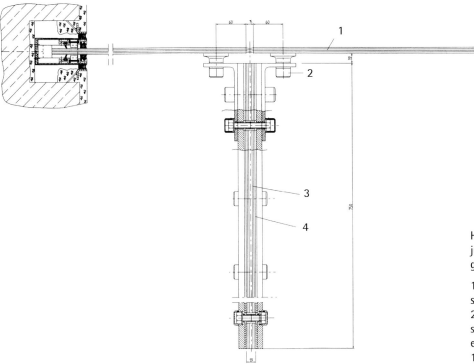

Horizontal section through junction of glass wall and glass stiffener, scale 1:10.

1 "Planar" system toughened safety glass, 12 mm.
2 "Planar 902" fixing for single glazing. 3 Glass stiffener, toughened safety glass, 19 mm. 4 EPDM, 3 mm.

Vertical sections through main façade, scale 1:50.

Detail of glass stiffener fixing: 1 Glass angle.
2 Sheet metal cladding.
3 Glass stiffener fixing made from stainless steel.
4 Glass stiffener.

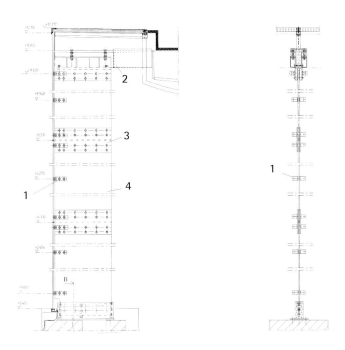

the eight floors of the museum and offers good views over the 4,000 m² of exhibition space, rising from the rock strata on which the city is founded, through the cellars of the Middle Ages, to the sections of the buildings dating from the 18th century used to display the salon furnishings of the 19th. The subterranean floors are devoted to the evolution of the city and historical events, whereas the upper floors document the social history of the city since the 19th century. Six carefully crafted wooden models, specially made for the museum, depict the story of the city's development from the 10th century, through the period as a fortified town to an open design following dismantling of the fortifications. Besides the exhibition rooms, the museum also has an auditorium, a documentation centre with library and archives, a "children's room" and a cafeteria on a garden terrace with splendid views across the deep River Alzette valley.

Connection between outer panes and glass stiffeners with individual fixings at the base.

Glass wall adjacent to the entrance. Elevation, vertical sections and plans, scale 1:150.

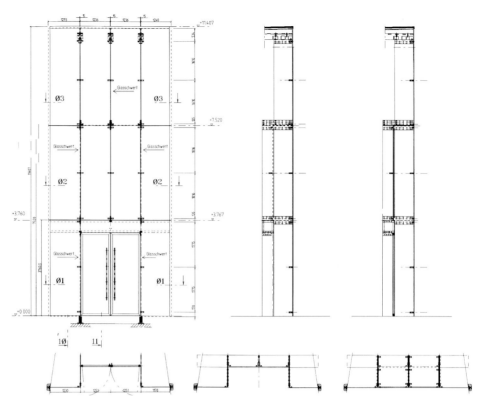

Vertical section through glass construction to reception hall, scale 1:150. The 12-m-high façade is made from 12 mm toughened safety glass using the "Planar" system. The panes, each 1.27 m wide and 3.76 m high, are mounted in groups of three, one above the other. Glass stiffeners made from 19 mm tough-ened safety glass serve to stabilize the vertical joints in the glass wall.

Roof plan, scale 1:150. The edges are glazed with lami-nated safety glass incorpor-ating "Infrastop neutral 51/38" solar-control glass.

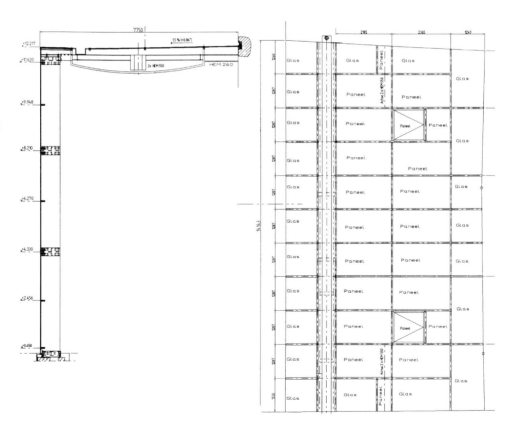

Fully glazed façades

The glass elevation, 12 m high and 14 m long, on the rue de Saint-Esprit in front of the reception area is made from toughened safety glass ("Delodur"), 12 mm thick, using the "Planar" system of individual screw fixings. The panes, each 1.27 m wide and 3.76 m high, are mounted in groups of three, one above the other. Glass stiffeners made of toughened safety glass, 19 mm thick, are attached at the vertical joints and lend stability. The three 750-mm-wide pieces of glass mounted one above the other to form each stiffener are connected by way of stainless steel plates screwed together. At the top, they are supported by cantilevered steel beams (HEM 260), at the bottom, they disappear into a plinth clad with sheet metal. As protection, the edge of the glass is covered by a plastic rail which extends to 3 m above the base. The individual screw fixings are attached to the glass stiffeners. Six of these fixings with countersunk head screws are used to hold each of the panes of the façade. The edges of the roof over the reception area are fully glazed so that the roof appears to float. In line with the regulations covering overhead glazing, the roof is made from laminated safety glass with solar-control properties; "Infrastop neutral 51/38" was chosen (light transmittance 51%, total energy transmittance 38%). The entrance elevation by the staircase tower employs a fully glazed wall fixed with the "Planar" system. The centre bay containing the twin leaves of the entrance door is set back from the others. A box-type beam forms the lintel over the door. The contemporary design of the entire glass front facing rue de Saint-Esprit complements the old buildings without obstructing the view of them. Depending on the direction of the light, the buildings across the narrow street are reflected in the glass wall. This design successfully illustrates how glass can be utilized in conjunction with listed buildings.

Plan, 2nd floor,
scale approx. 1:1200:
Russian–Roman steam baths
with hot-water (36°C) and
cold-water (18°C) pools,
Finnish sauna with plunge
pool (16°C).

148

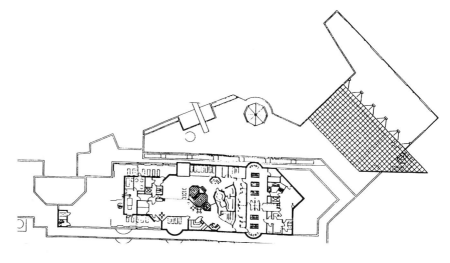

Plan, 1st floor,
scale approx. 1:1200:
curative media department,
treatment rooms, kinesitherapy centre, kinesitherapy
pool (36°C), lecture theatre,
management offices.

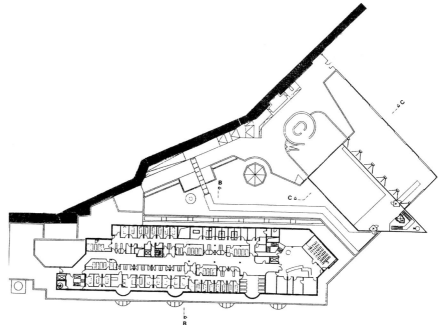

Plan, ground floor,
scale approx. 1:1200:
entrance foyer, cafeteria,
changing rooms, indoor
swimming pool (276 m^2)
and outdoor pool (191 m^2),
connected by a channel
through which pool users
swim.

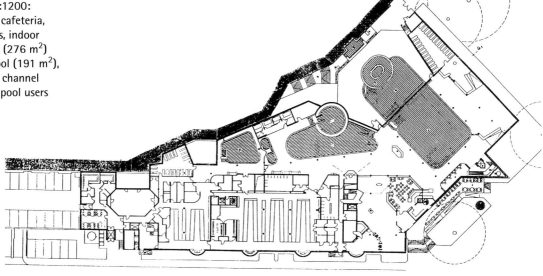

Entrance beneath suspended glass canopy made from 24 mm laminated safety glass comprising two panes of zone-toughened glass.

Thermal and mineral baths, Stuttgart–Bad Cannstadt
Beck-Erlang + Partner

Bad Cannstadt, until 1905 an independent town, is today incorporated into the city of Stuttgart. With 18 springs, supplying 18 million litres of mineral water daily, Bad Cannstadt is one of the largest sources of mineral water in Europe. The medicinal benefits of this water were already known to the Romans, who erected a fortress here. In the centre of the old spa town, with its classical-style architecture, stands the medical administration and treatment building (*Kurhaus*), built in 1825-26 to a design by Nicolaus Friedrich von Thouret. The municipal mineral baths were erected next to this around the turn of the century and re-established in a makeshift manner following severe damage during the Second World War. Indeed, the area in the immediate vicinity of the *Kurhaus* remained neglected for many years. Therefore, the 1980 urban planning competition was intended to inject fresh, new life into this health resort.

The best entry in the competition was judged to be that of Beck-Erlang & Partner, with an arena-like pool landscape on the edge of the slope of the park. It offered a relaxing and private atmosphere –after all, the thermal and mineral baths are not meant to be a bustling leisure facility but rather a place for recuperation and therapy. The new building is set back from the neighbouring *Kurhaus*, rising up behind the garden forecourt. It juts out towards the roadway and thus creates its own entrance zone. Visitors pass under a suspended, fully glazed canopy, providing protection for the terrace cafeteria accessible from both inside and outside, and straightaway get a view of the entire baths through the glass wall in the entrance foyer. The sculptor Helmut Pizzinini from Florence collaborated with the architects on the artistic concept involving fountains and colours. All the large mineral and thermal baths are on the same level as the entrance foyer. The large pool is joined to an outside pool, overlooked by the sunbathing terraces on the slope of the park.

Mineral water and thermal salt-water baths
The swimming, bathing and therapy pools contain different types of water at different temperatures. Available are the indoor swimming pool (276 m²) and outdoor pool (191 m²), connected by a channel through which pool users swim, as well as two hot whirlpools with thermal salt-water at 36°C, a warm circular pool near the

Location
Mineralbad Cannstadt,
Sulzerrainstrasse 2,
70372 Stuttgart, Germany

Client
Stuttgart local authority

Architects
Beck-Erlang + Partner,
Stuttgart

Wilfried Beck-Erlang, Brigitte
Schopf, Gunther Baacke

Project Manager
Brigitte Schopf

Structural engineers
Ing.-Gesellschaft für Bauwesen
GbR, Meyer-Vorfelder &
Dinkelacker, Sindelfingen

Structural design of
parabolic roof
Schlaich, Bergermann &
Partner, Stuttgart

Project Manager
H. Schober

Landscape architects
Geiger/Bässler, Stuttgart

Fountains and colour concept
Helmut Pizzinini, Florence

Glass construction
Helmut Fischer GmbH, Talheim

Date of completion
1995

steam baths on the second floor, and multipurpose indoor and outdoor pools. Wilhelm spring water at approx. 18°C is available in the cold-water pool on the ground floor and next to the steam baths on the second floor. All pools are drained and cleaned every evening, and refilled overnight.

Lattice barrel-vault roof

A glass roof with galvanized supporting steelwork covers the 10 x 16 m salt-water swimming pool. The parabolic shell of the roof points towards the road at 45° like the bow of a ship. It covers a trapezoidal plan shape, 15 m wide and 22/35 m long with a 5.3 m rise. The steelwork is arranged as a right-angled lattice of solid steel flats, 40 and 60 mm thick, 1000 to 1400 mm long. This delicate grid of steel is shaped like a slightly asymmetrical parabolic lattice barrel-vault. To achieve this, the supporting arches had to be reinforced by three pretensioned groups of cables in a radial arrangement at 10.6 m centres. This project marked the first use of flat insulating glass laid directly on a parabolic roof surface.

"Infrastop Silber 50/35" solar-control insulating glass was employed: 6 mm float glass outer pane, 12 mm cavity, 8 mm laminated safety glass inner pane with a silver-blue tint. The glass has a U value of 1.4 W/m^{2}K, a light transmittance of 50% and a total energy transmittance of 35%. The joints between the panes are sealed flush with permanently elastic silicone. Circular "patch" fittings at each corner of every pane provide a mechanical means of resisting uplift due to wind suction. The right-angled mesh of the supporting structure is stabilized by pretensioned diagonal cables. Both gables of the hall as well as the side walls are composed of column-and-beam arrangements of rectangular hollow sections, 120 x 60 mm, spaced to match the roof lattice.

Structural design for parabolic roof.

System, longitudinal section.

Cross-section, rooftop view.

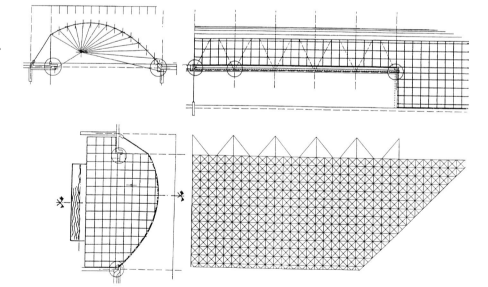

Swimming pool hall beneath parabolic roof. A channel leads to the outdoor pool. Radial arrangements of pretensioned cables stabilize the parabolic shell.

Lift and stairs at the corner of the glass hall.

The new facilities on the slope of the park adjoin the garden terrace in front of the classical-style *Kurhaus*.

Transition from glass roof to gable wall with exit to rooftop terrace.

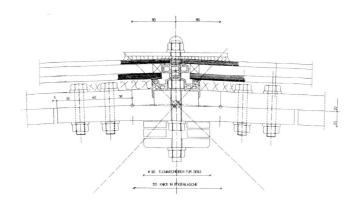

Section through node point on parabolic roof, scale approx. 1:5. Circular glass "patch" fitting for mechanical anchorage. Glazing: "Infrastop Silber 50/35" solar-control insulating glass (6 mm float glass outer pane, 12 mm cavity, 8 mm laminated safety glass inner pane, U value 1.4 W/m²K).

Index

Acknowledgements

All illustrations, except those by the author as mentioned below, are courtesy of the architects, engineers and clients.

Bauwelt, Berlin (D): 117, 120 l.

Benthem Crouwel, Amsterdam (NL): 26, 27.

Brüder Eckelt + Co. Steyr (A): 30 rt + rb, 32–33, 60–62.

Deutsches Museum, München (D): 9 b.

Hans Ege, Luzern (CH): 2, 111, 114.

Helmut Fischer GmbH, Talheim (D): 65, 85, 87, 93–95.

Josef Gartner + Co. Gundelfingen (D): 47, 48, 96, 99, 100, 101, 105, 108, 122, 123, 125, 127, 129.

Denis Gilbert, London (GB): 70–72.

Glas Marte GmbH, Bregenz (A): 113.

von Gerkan, Marg und Partner, Hamburg (D): 131–133.

Marianne Götz, Stuttgart (D): 151 rt + rb.

GÖTZ GmbH, Würzburg (D): 74, 75, 77–79.

Guido Gremler, Paris (F): 42 tl + br, 43.

Heinz W. Krewinkel, Böblingen (D): 11, 23, 25, 29, 30 tr, 35, 37, 38, 51, 52, 67, 81–83, 86, 89–91, 102, 103, 140 bl, 146.

Otto Mair, Staben (I): 22 r.

Paul Ott, Graz (A): 13–16.

Pilkington Flachglas AG, Gelsenkirchen (D): 66, 67, 69, 143, 144, 149, 151 lt + b.

Pilkington plc, St Helens (GB): 6.

Ines Schöttle, Sindelfingen (D): 18, 19, 22 l + m, 137, 139, 140 tl + r.

Seele GmbH, Gersthofen (D): 134, 135.

SNCF, Paris (F): 41, 42 tr.

Rafael Viñoly, New York NY (USA): 120 rt + b, 121.

Valentin Wormbs, Stuttgart (D): 55, 56.